The Story of Catherine Booth

For Young People

by
Colonel Mildred Duff

Preface by
General Bramwell Booth

Schmul Publishing Company
Nicholasville, Kentucky

Published by Schmul Publishing Co.
PO Box 776
Nicholasville, KY USA

Printed in the United States of America

ISBN 10: 0-88019-112-0
ISBN 13: 978-0-88019-112-8

PREFACE

Colonel Duff has, at my request, written the following very interesting and touching account of my dear Mother; and she has done so in the hope that those who read it will be helped to follow in the footsteps of that wonderful servant of God.

But how can they do so? Was not Mrs. Booth, you ask, an exceptional woman? Had she not great gifts and very remarkable powers, and was she not trained in a very special way to do the work to which God called her? How, then, can ordinary people follow in her steps? Let me tell you.

Mrs. Booth walked with God. When she was only a timid girl, helping her mother in the household, she continually sought after Him; and when, in later years, she became known by multitudes, and was written of in the newspapers, and greatly beloved by the good in many lands, there was no difference in her life in that matter. She was not content with being Mrs. General Booth of The Salvation Army, and with being looked upon as a great and good woman, giving her life to bless others. No! she listened daily for God's voice in her own heart, sought after His will, and leaned continually for strength and grace upon her Saviour. You can be like her in that.

Mrs. Booth was a soul-winner. A little while before her spirit passed into the presence of God, and when she knew that death was quite near to her, she said: 'Tell the Soldiers that the great consolation for a Salvationist on his dying bed is to feel that he has been a soul-winner.' Wherever she went—in the houses of strangers as well as of friends, in the Meetings, great and small, when she was welcomed and when she was not, whether alone or with others—she laboured to lead souls to Christ. I have known her at one time spend as much trouble to win one as at another time to win fifty. You can follow her example in that.

Mrs. Booth always declared herself and took sides with right. Whatever was happening around her, people always knew which side she was on. She spoke out for the right, the good, and the true, even when doing so involved very disagreeable experiences and the bearing of much unkindness. She hated the spirit which can look on at what is wicked and false or cruel, and say, 'Oh, that is not my affair!' You can follow her example in this also.

Mrs. Booth laboured all her life to improve her gifts. She thought; she prayed; she worked; she read—above all, she read her Bible. It was her companion as a child, as a young follower of Christ, and then as a Leader in The Army. Those miserable words which some of us hear so often about some bad or unfinished work—'Oh, that will do'—were seldom heard from her lips. She was always striving, striving, striving to do better, and yet better, and again better still. All this also you can do.

Mrs. Booth was full of sympathy. No one who was in need or in sorrow, or who was suffering, could meet her without finding out that she was in sympathy with them. Her heart was tender with the love of Christ, and so she was deeply touched by the sin and sorrow around her just as He was. Even the miseries of the dumb animals moved her to efforts on their behalf. This sympathy made Mrs. Booth quick to see and appreciate the toil and self-denial of others, and ever grateful for any kindness shown to her or to The Army or to those in need of any kind. The very humblest and youngest of those who read this little book can be like her in all this.

Mrs. Booth endured to the end. She never turned back. She was faithful. Her life and work would have been spoilt if she had given up the fight. She was often sorely tempted. She was slandered and misrepresented by enemies, betrayed by false friends, and often deeply wounded by those who professed to love her, though they deserted the Flag. But she held fast. You can be like her in that. You may make many mistakes, suffer many defeats, but you can still keep going on, and it is to those who go on to the very end, whether in weakness or in strength, that Jesus will give the crown of life.

Mrs. Booth trusted with all her heart in the love and sacrifice of her Saviour. These were her hope and her strength. When at the height of her influence and popularity she delighted in that wonderful song which we still so often sing :—

> I love Thee because Thou hast first lovèd me,
> And purchased my pardon when nailed to the tree ;

and when, amid much suffering, she lay dying, we often sang together with her:—

Victory for me!
Through the Blood of Christ my Saviour;
Victory for me!
Through the precious Blood.

This was her victory. You can follow her in the faith that won it. Will you?

BRAMWELL BOOTH.

International Headquarters.

CATHERINE BOOTH:

A SKETCH

I

CHILDHOOD

'Parents who love God best will not allow their children to learn anything which could not be pressed into His service.'—MRS. BOOTH.

THE Mother of The Salvation Army was born at Ashbourne, in Derbyshire, on January 17, 1829, and God gave to her the very best gift He can give to any child—a good and holy mother.

Katie Mumford, as she was then called, had no sister to play with, and of her four brothers only one lived to be a man. But her dear mother more than made up for every lack, and from her lips the little girl learned those blessed lessons which, in her turn, she has taught to us.

One lesson which Mrs. Mumford early taught her daughter was that our bodies will not live for ever. She took Katie to see the body of her infant brother who had just died; and, though she was not more than two years old at the time, Katie never forgot that first lesson. Spiritual things were even then real to her, just because they were so real to her mother. Heaven was home to her, and Jesus her best Friend, ever near to help and guide her.

Truthfulness was a second of those early lessons which remained with our Army Mother all her life. She was but four years old when Mrs. Mumford found her one evening sobbing bitterly in her little cot long after she should have been asleep. She had told a falsehood, and conscience would not let her rest. When she had sobbed out her confession, her mother talked and prayed with her, and at last left her, happy in the assurance that she was forgiven by her Heavenly Father.

After this you will not be surprised to hear that another lesson early taught to Katie by her mother was to love her Bible. She could read nicely when she was but five years old, and she loved to stand by her mother's side, and read the Bible stories aloud, with just a little help over the very long words. And this love for God's Word grew deeper every year, so that by the time she was twelve years old she had read it through eight times. In later years people often wondered how it was that Mrs. Booth knew her Bible so well, and could so quickly answer their difficulties and objections in Bible words. Much of the secret lay in this early training, and in the hours she spent in Bible study later on, when she had reached the age of some of our younger Corps Cadets.

I wish we could have seen her in those days. She had very dark hair, which curled naturally; black, flashing eyes, and such a warm heart, and strong, impetuous nature that she could do nothing by halves. Whatever it was, work or play, her whole soul had to be in it.

Since she was not at all strong, and had few girl friends, Katie did not play rough or noisy games, but her love for her dolls made her quite a little mother to them. She treated them almost like real children, and would sew and toil, and never rest till she felt she had in every way done her duty to them. She loved animals, too, especially dogs and horses, and could not bear to see any one ill-treat them. Oh, how she suffered one day, watching some poor sheep driven down the road! She watched the man beat them—she could not stop him; and at last she tore home, and flung herself down almost choking and speechless with indignation and distress.

Her mother did not check Katie for feeling so keenly. She encouraged her; for she knew that a hard, indifferent child, who can see suffering and not care or be distressed over it, would make a hard woman; and she wanted her Katie to be full of love and tenderness for all, and especially for those needing help.

When Catherine was twelve years old she became very interested in the drink question. She wrote letters about it, and sent them to different newspapers, for there was no 'War Cry' nor 'Young Soldier' in those days; and she also became the secretary of what was then called a Juvenile Temperance Society, and did all she could to get boys and girls to promise never to touch the drink.

Katie was also, like many of you, much

interested in the heathen. She would go round to all her friends collecting money to pay for preachers to be sent to them; and in order to get more money she would deny herself sugar and other small luxuries. No one told Katie to do this; but you see our Army Mother herself taught us, by her example when only a child, to keep our great Self-Denial Week.

Of course, most of Katie's time was taken up with her lessons, and, as she loved to learn and study, they were no hardship to her. For two years she went to a boarding-school, and here her companions soon found out how straight and truthful she was. 'You'll never get *her* to tell a lie,' the girls said, 'nor even to exaggerate, so it's no use trying.' Every one knew also that Katie felt for the backward girls and those who were slow and dull. She wanted them to succeed, and would help them between school hours. That was her joy, you see—to help and care for others; whether at school or at home she was the same.

But you must not think that Catherine was perfect. Oh, no, indeed! Sometimes her schoolmates would tease her because she was so quiet, and liked to read better than to play; and at such times, instead of being patient, she would flare up into a passion, and say harsh, angry words. When the storm was over she would be, however, Oh! so sorry, and would beg her schoolfellows to forgive her.

When Katie had been at school two years, God sent her a very great trial. Instead of being able to go on learning and keeping up with the other girls, she had to return home, and for three long years to lie nearly all the time on her back, often suffering very much. She had a serious spinal complaint, and her friends sometimes doubted whether she would ever walk again.

You wonder what she did in those three years? I will tell you. When the pain would permit it, she would knit and sew. She could not, of course, hold heavy needlework; but little things, like babies' socks and hoods, pin-cushions, and so forth, she would make most beautifully, and then they would be sold to help on the work of God.

Besides her sewing, Katie read a great deal. First, as I have already told you, she read her Bible, and learnt to know God's thoughts about the world and sin, and His wishes for His people. For seven months at one time Catherine had to lie on her face on a special sort of couch made on purpose for her; but she invented a contrivance by which, even then, she could read her Bible, though still remaining in the position that the doctors wished. Then, too, she would read good books—explanations of the Bible, about Holiness, soul-saving, lives of those who have lived and worked for God, and so on. When she had read a chapter she would shut the book, and write down as much as she could remember of it. This helped her to think clearly and to remember what she read, and also to put her thoughts into words.

But she never wasted her time reading stories and novels. Later on in her life she said she was so thankful for this, for she thought that novels and silly story books made people discontented with their own homes and duties, and put wrong, hurtful ideas into their minds. Let us recollect and follow our Army Mother's example here, and not waste time on stories which are not true.

We, if we had known Katie Mumford in those three years of pain and weariness, should have pitied her very much. We might have been tempted to feel that God was hard in not letting her be strong like other girls; but we now see that all the time He was fitting her for the wonderful future before her; and when she became Mrs. Booth, the great preacher, she herself understood this.

'Being so much alone in my youth,' she said, 'and so thrown on my own thoughts and on those expressed in books, has been very helpful to me. Had I been given to gossip, and had there been people for me to gossip with, I should certainly never have accomplished what I did.'

So, you see, God was all the time giving her the very best training He could, and teaching her, as she lay there alone on her bed, what she never could have learned in the ordinary way. And He will train you, too, in the very best way for your future, if you will but determine to trust and serve Him as did Catherine Mumford.

II

CONVERSION AND SOUL STRUGGLES

'No soul was ever yet saved who was too idle to seek.'—MRS. BOOTH.

PERHAPS you, the Corps Cadet, for whom I am especially writing this little book, have been tempted to break your vows by becoming engaged to some one who does not want to be an Officer. And you think, perhaps, that no one understands your feelings.

You will be surprised, then, to know that our Army Mother had just such a battle to fight when she was a girl.

She had a cousin, a little older than herself, who was tall and very clever. He came with his parents to stay in her home, and Katie had not seen him since they were young children. He quickly grew very fond of his cousin, and Catherine found how nice it was to have some one to give her presents and to love her as he did. At last he begged her to promise that by and by she would be engaged to him. Now Katie was very perplexed. On the one hand she loved her cousin, and did not want to grieve him, and yet in her heart she knew he was not truly given up to God, and would not help her in her soul.

'Go to the Meeting with you, Katie?' he used to say. 'Of course, I'll go anywhere to please you.' But then, while she was trying to get a blessing, he would be scratching little pictures on the back of the seat to make her laugh. Perhaps you can guess the struggle it was for Katie to decide what her answer should be. 'If you will only say "yes," and be engaged to him, I am sure you will be able to help him, and very likely get him properly saved,' the Devil would whisper. 'Break it off now, Katie; do not go another step; you know God cannot smile on it.' That was how her conscience spoke.

At last, one day as she was truly praying and seeking for light, she read the verse in 2 Corinthians vi. 14: 'Be ye not unequally yoked together with unbelievers.' It came to her as the voice of God.

'I will do it, Lord,' she said, after a long struggle; and she sat down, and wrote her cousin a letter, telling him just why she could never be engaged to him, and breaking it all off for ever. Then she turned back to her home duties, and did not re-open the question.

And did our Army Mother in after years regret that she had acted like this? No, indeed; she has told us that she saw plainly later on that, if just then she had chosen to follow her own feelings and wishes, instead of obeying God's command, all her life would have been altered, and she would never have done the glorious work He had planned for her. It was a hard battle at the time, and cost her many tears; but it was worth it, ten thousand times over, as we can all see to-day.

Very soon after this victory Catherine became really converted.

'What!' you say. 'Was she not converted before this?'

No. All her life she had, like many children trained to-day in Salvationist homes, felt God's Holy Spirit striving with her. Sometimes, when quite a little girl, her mother would find her crying because she felt how she had sinned against God.

But when she was about fifteen she longed to know that she was really saved.

'Don't be silly,' said the Devil in her heart. 'You have been as good as saved all your life. You have always wanted to do right. How can you expect such a sudden change as if you were a great big drunkard? It's absurd.'

'But my *heart* is as bad as the heart of a big sinner,' cried poor Katie in an agony of fear. 'I have been as bad inside, if not in my outward actions and words.'

And then she took hold of God in faith. 'Lord, I *must* be converted. I cannot rest till Thou hast changed my whole nature; do for me what Thou dost do for the thieves and drunkards.'

But for six weeks it seemed as if God did not hear her cry. She grew more and more unhappy. All her past sins rose before her: those bursts of temper when she was at school, those wrong thoughts and feelings. Yes, the Bible was true when it said: 'The heart is deceitful above all things and desperately wicked.'

Katie argued, too, like this: 'I cannot recollect any time or place where I claimed Salvation and the forgiveness of my sins; if God *has* saved me, He would surely have made me certain of it. Anyway, I must and will know it. I must have the assurance that I am God's child.'

Unable to rest, she would pace her room till two o'clock in the morning, and would lie down at last, with her Bible and hymn-book under her pillow, praying that God would Himself tell her that her sins were forgiven. At last, one morning, as she woke, she opened her hymn-book, and read these words:—

My God, I am Thine,
What a comfort divine,
What a blessing to know that my Jesus is mine.

Now she had read and sung these lines scores of times before, but they came this morning with a new power to her soul.

'I am Thine!' 'My Jesus is mine!' she exclaimed. 'Lord, it is true!—I do believe it! My sins are forgiven. I belong to Thee!' and her whole soul was filled with light and joy. She now possessed what she had been seeking all these weeks—the assurance of Salvation! And then what do you think she did? She threw on a wrapper, and, without waiting to dress, hurried across to her mother's room, and tapped at the door.

'Come in,' said her mother's voice; and Katie, her face shining with joy, burst into the room. 'Mamma, mamma, I am a child of God! My sins are forgiven—Jesus is my Saviour!' she cried, flinging herself into her mother's arms. And this was the same Katie, who had been so shy and backward that she had never before dared to speak about her spiritual anxieties, even to her mother! Ah! what a change real conversion, or change of heart, had made.

For the next six months Katie was so happy that she felt as if she were walking on air. 'I used to tremble,' she tells us, 'and even long to die, lest I should backslide or lose the sense of God's favour.'

But as time went on she learned, as we all have to do, to walk by faith, not by sight, and to serve and follow the Saviour whether she had happy feelings or not.

But you must not suppose, because Katie had the assurance of Salvation, that therefore she had no more fighting. No—indeed, her fighting days had only just begun.

One of her great difficulties, which many Corps Cadets will understand, was that she felt so nervous about doing anything in public. No one, of course, asked her to speak—such a thing was never dreamed of; but the lady who took the Bible Class which she attended regularly would now and then ask her to pray. 'Miss Mumford will pray,' the lady would say, when they were all kneeling together.

But Katie was too shy to begin, and sometimes they would wait for several minutes before she had courage to say a few words. 'Don't ask me to pray again,' she said one day to her leader; 'the excitement and agitation make me quite ill.'

'I can't help that,' was the very wise answer; 'you must break through your timidity; for otherwise you will be of no use to God.'

And did Katie persevere? Yes, indeed, she did. Here is an entry made some time later in the diary that she kept, which shows you how very much her experience was like yours:—

'I have not been blessed so much for weeks as I was to-night. I prayed aloud. The cross was great, but so was the reward.

My heart beat violently, but I felt some liberty.'

Though Catherine's spine difficulty was better, she was still very delicate, and at the age of eighteen every one felt sure she was going into a decline. But, sick or well, her soul grew stronger, and her desire to please and serve God better increased every day.

'I do love Thee,' she wrote in the same little diary, 'but I want to love Thee more.'

It was not till many years later that Catherine received the blessing of a clean heart; but even now she had begun to desire and long for it. She also writes at this time: 'I see that this Full Salvation is very necessary if I am to glorify God below, and find my way to Heaven. I want a *clean* heart. Lord, take me and seal me.'

Some people, even after they are converted, are too proud to own themselves wrong, or to confess when they have sinned. Catherine was not of that sort. In one of her letters to her mother she ends with these words:—

'Pray for me, dear mother, and believe me, with all my faults and besetments, your loving child.'

Her hunger after a holy life was real and practical. She knew she must learn to live by method—that is, doing right, whether she liked it or not—and not by feelings, if she was to be of use in the world.

So at the end of the year she wrote some new resolutions; and as they may be of help to you, I will copy them for you just as she put them down:—

'I have been writing a few daily rules for the coming year, which I hope will prove a blessing to me, by the grace of God. I have got a paper of printed rules also, which I intend to read once a week. May the Lord help me to keep to them! But, above all, I am determined to search the Scriptures more attentively, for in them I have eternal life. I have read my Bible through twice during the past sixteen months, but I must read it with more prayer for light and understanding. Oh, may it be my meat and drink! May I meditate on it day and night! And then I shall bring forth fruit in season; my leaf also shall not wither, and whatsoever I do shall prosper.'

She had also her own private ways of denying herself, not for the sake of earning money or praise by it, but simply because she felt it was right. One of these rules was to do without dinner, and butter at breakfast, once in the week, because she felt it helped her in her soul.

I cannot end this chapter without telling you of the one great sorrow which darkened all her early years. Some of you, I know, will enter into her feelings so well.

Her father, at one time saved and earnest about the souls of others, had grown cold and backslidden, and now never even went near a Meeting. You can fancy what agony this was to both Mrs. Mumford and her daughter. They prayed and wept in vain —he only seemed to get more indifferent. Catherine would sometimes write her feelings and her sorrow in her diary, and there we read:—

'I sometimes get into an agony of feeling while praying for my dear father. Oh, my Lord, answer prayer, and bring him back to Thyself! Never let that tongue which once delighted in praising Thee, and in showing others Thy willingness to save, be engaged in uttering the lamentations of the lost! Oh, awful thought! Lord, have mercy! Save, Oh! save him in any way Thou seest best, though it be ever so painful. If by removing me Thou canst do this, cut short Thy work, and take me Home. Let me be bold to speak in Thy name. Oh, give me true courage and liberty, and when I write to him, bless what I say to the good of his soul!'

For many years this prayer of Catherine's was not answered; but she held on, as you must do for those you love, in faith and prayer; and at last she had the unspeakable joy of seeing her dear father come back to God through one of her own Meetings which he had attended. His last years were full of peace, and were spent in serving God and rejoicing in His Salvation.

III

A THREE-YEARS ENGAGEMENT

'What a need there is for effort and energy; or real religion and common sense!'—MRS. BOOTH.

ONE Sunday, when Catherine and her mother went to the Meeting as usual, they found a 'Special' there, taking the services. He was quite different from the other Specials, and Catherine could not help noticing him with extra interest. He spoke to the people's hearts, and was not so much occupied in preaching a good sermon as in getting some one converted. But he did preach a very good sermon for all that, and chose this verse as his text—'This is indeed the Christ, the Saviour of the world.'

A few days later Catherine and her mother were spending the evening with a friend, when the very same preacher came in, and was introduced to them as the Rev. William Booth.

Catherine knew they had one subject in common—love for souls; but before the evening ended she discovered that the young minister was quite as earnest as she was herself in fighting the Drink curse and all that was connected with it.

A few Sundays later Mr. Booth preached again in the same building, this time as the minister, or, as we should say, 'Officer in charge,' and no longer as a Special. And now you will guess that the two often met, and that, because they had so many interests in common, they soon learned to know each other well, till respect grew into friendship, and friendship into love.

Catherine was at this time twenty-two years old, and Mr. Booth was three months younger; but, though you would have said they were old enough to know their own minds, they did nothing hastily, and would enter into no engagement till they were quite sure of God's Will in the matter.

Had Catherine ever before thought of the day when she would get married? you, perhaps, ask. Oh, yes, indeed, and when but a girl of sixteen—directly, in fact, after she was saved—she settled in her own heart what sort of a man her future husband must be. First, she decided, he must be truly converted, and a total abstainer, not to please her, but from his own choice. Then he must be a man of sense, or she could never respect him; and, if they were to be happy, they must feel and think alike on all important matters.

Ah, if our women-Soldiers and Cadets to-day would but follow our Army Mother's example, there would be fewer unhappy marriages and wrecked lives!

But in her secret heart Catherine had also, girl-like, some ideas about the sort of man she would like to marry, if she might choose. He should be a minister—that was the nearest she could get to an Officer in those days; William was a name she particularly liked, and—if only he might be tall and dark! If you had been there when Katie Mumford first listened to his preaching you would have seen that he was 'tall and dark' indeed.

But though William Booth loved Catherine with a deep and holy love, which increased each time they met, yet he was very poor, and he wondered if he ought, under the circumstances, to ask her to share his lot. He wrote a letter to her, telling her how perplexed and troubled he was, and her answer shows us that, right from the very earliest days, before they were even engaged, her one desire was that his soul should prosper.

'My dear friend,' she begins . . . 'The thought that I should cause you any suffering or increase your perplexity is almost unbearable. I am tempted to wish that we had never seen each other. Do try to forget me, as far as the remembrance would injure your usefulness or spoil your peace. If I have no alternative but to oppose the Will of God, or trample on the desolations of my own heart, *my choice is made.* "Thy will be done" is my constant cry. I care not for myself; but Oh, if I cause you to err, I shall never be happy again.'

It was not the fear of poverty that frightened her, for a few days later she says:—

'I fear you did not fully understand my difficulty. It was not circumstances. I thought I had assured you that a bright prospect would not allure me, nor a dark one affright me, if only we are *one in heart.*

My only reason for wishing to defer the engagement was that *you* might feel satisfied in your mind that the step is right. . . . If you are convinced on this point, let circumstances go, and let us be one, come what may.'

This is exactly what they did, and after meeting, and together consecrating their lives to God, they solemnly pledged themselves to each other.

And now began a three-years' engagement, in which, though often for long months at a time they never met, they remained true to each other and to God, in thought and word and deed.

Many of the beautiful letters that our Army Mother wrote to The General at this time, I am glad to tell you, have been kept, and we will look together at some of the ways in which she tried to help and cheer him.

In the first letter after their engagement she ends with these words:—

'The more you lead me up to Christ in all things, the more highly shall I esteem you; and if it be possible to love you more than I do now, the more shall I love you. You are always present in my thoughts.'

Now you must not think that, even in these early days, our General had a very easy life. He was often much perplexed and troubled, longing above all to do God's Will for the Salvation of the people, and yet not quite sure what that Will was. At these times Catherine was of untold help to him.

Once he was very unsettled—not certain whether he should remain away in the North of England, or accept a place in London, where the two could often meet. Most girls would have said, 'Oh, come, then we shall be near to each other'; but you will see that her advice to him is just as suitable for you when you are not certain of your duty—that she does not consider her own feelings at all.

'I wish,' she writes, 'you prayed more and talked less about the matter. Try it, and be determined to get clear and settled views as to your course. Leave your heart before God, and get satisfied in His sight, and then do it, be it what it may. I cannot bear the idea of your being unhappy. Pray do in this as you feel in your soul it will be right. My conscience is no standard for yours.'

Then she adds, lower down:—

'Oh, if you come to London, let us be determined to reap a blessed harvest. Let our fellowship be sanctified to our souls' everlasting good. My mind is made up to do my part towards it. I hope to be firm as a rock on some points. The Lord help me. We must aim to improve each other's mind and character. Let us pray for grace to do it in the best way and to the fullest extent possible.'

'Anyway,' she says, a day or two later—and ever remember her words when outside things try and distress you—'don't let the controversy hurt your soul. Live near to God by prayer. . . . You believe He answers prayer. Then take courage. Just fall down at His feet, and open your very soul before Him, and throw yourself right into His arms. Tell Him that if you are wrong you only wait to be set right, and, be the path rough or smooth, you will walk in it.

'Oh, you must live close to God! If you are a greater distance from Him than you were, just stop the whirl of outward things, or rather leave it, and shut yourself up with Him till all is clear and bright upwards. Do, there's a dear. Oh, how much we lose by not coming to the point. Now, at once, realize your union with Christ, and trust Him to lead you through this perplexity. Bless you. Excuse this advice. I am anxious for your soul. Look up. If God hears my prayers, He must guide you —He will guide you.'

In these early days our General was tempted, as some of us are tempted to-day, to feel nervous and shy when talking before large crowds, and where the people were better dressed and better off than usual. He wrote his feelings to Catherine, and she sends him back her wise advice and help.

'I am sorry for this,' she says, 'and am persuaded it is the fear of man which shackles you. Do not give place to this feeling. Remember you are *the Lord's servant*, and if you are a faithful one it will be a small matter with you to be judged of man's judgment. Let nothing be wanting beforehand to make what you say helpful, but when you are before the people try to think only of your own responsibility to Him who hath sent you.'

Again, later, she writes:—

'Try and cast off the fear of man. Fix your eyes simply on the glory of God, and care not for frown or praise of man. Rest not till your soul is fully alive to God.'

How truly she herself carried this out in her own Meetings you will hear later on.

Miss Mumford was very anxious that The General should improve himself with plenty of hard work. She saw what he might become, and she also knew that unless he did *his* part all those wonderful powers which God had lent to him would be thrown away.

'Do assure me,' she writes, 'my own dear William, that no want of energy or effort on your part shall hinder the improvement of those talents God has given you.'

So that, with his constant travelling and preaching, he might get time to read and think and learn, she suggested a little plan to him in his billets.

Could you not,' she says, 'provide yourself with a small leather bag or case, large enough to hold your Bible and any other book you might require—pens, ink, paper and a candle? And, presuming that you generally have a room to yourself, could you not rise by six o'clock every morning, and convert your bedroom into a study till breakfast time? . . . I hope, my dearest love, you will consider this plan, and keep to it, if possible, as a general practice. Don't let little difficulties prevent your carrying it out.'

You must remember that at this time neither Catherine nor Mr. Booth ever dreamed of the wonderful work they were to be called to do. He was then preaching and getting souls saved, mostly in country places, and had many a 'hard go,' but *that* was no reason why he should not improve.

Did The General like this advice and counsel? Or did he feel, as some men do to-day, that women cannot judge nor understand such things?

Ah! he was wise, and only too glad to have all the help that Catherine could give him. In fact, he often wrote begging her to help him more. The outlines for addresses which she sent him weekly he valued and used, as this letter shows:—

'I have,' he writes, 'just taken hold of that sketch you sent me on "Be not deceived," and am about to make a full sermon on it. I like it much. It is admirable.

'I want a sermon on the Flood, one on Jonah, and one on the Judgment. Send me some bare thoughts, some clear, startling outlines. We must have that kind of truth which will move sinners.'

But if Catherine Mumford was anxious about the mind and work of her future husband, much more was she anxious about his soul. To her, there could be no true love without faithfulness, and where she felt it necessary, she cautioned him in the truest and tenderest way:—

'You have special need,' she writes, 'for watchfulness and for much private intercourse with God.

'My dearest love, beware how you indulge that dangerous element of character, ambition. Misdirected, it will be everlasting ruin to yourself, and perhaps to me also. Oh, my love, let nothing earthly excite it; let not the wish to be great fire it. Fix it on the Throne of the Eternal, and let it find the realization of its loftiest aspirations in the promotion of His glory, and it shall be consummated with the richest enjoyments and brightest glories of God's own Heaven.'

You wonder, perhaps, if Catherine ever wrote 'love letters,' as we call them. She never wrote the foolish and sentimental letters which say a great deal, and mean very little; but she was able to put her great love into words strong, intense, and full of tenderness.

'Do I remember?' she asks in one letter. 'Yes, I remember all—all that has bound us together. All the bright and happy, as well as the clouded and sorrowful times of our fellowship. Nothing relating to you can time or place erase from my memory. Your words, your looks, your actions, even the most trivial and incidental, come up before me as fresh as life. If I meet a child called William, I am more interested in him than in any other. Bless you. Keep your spirits up, and hope much for the future. God lives and loves us, and we shall be one in Him, loving each other as Christ loved us.'

William Booth and Catherine Mumford were married in London, on June 15, 1855; and here are a few lines from the last letter she wrote to him before the engagement was ended, and the long thirty-five years of happy married life began:—

'I long to see you. Your letters do not satisfy the yearnings of my heart. Perhaps they ought to. I wish it were differently constituted. I might be much happier. But it *will* be extravagant and enthusiastic in spite of all my schooling. If I ever get to Heaven, what rapture shall I know! No, there is no fear of our loving each other too much. How can we love each other more than Christ has loved us? And this is the standard He has given us. What a precious thing is the religion of Jesus! It makes our first duties our highest happiness. It has the promise of the life that now is, as well as of that which is to come. We will spend all our energies in trying to persuade men to receive and practise it.'

How wonderfully she carried this intention into practice, and, together with The General, lived every moment 'publishing the Sinner's Friend,' you shall read later on.

IV

A LIFE OF SACRIFICE

'Since I came to the crucifixion of myself, I have not cared much what men might say of me.' —MRS. BOOTH.

AT the time when our Army Mother married The General's work was, as we have seen, that of an 'Evangelist' or 'Travelling Minister.' He would stay in a town for some weeks or months, as the case might be, preaching and holding Meetings, and getting people saved, both in the town itself and the places round.

It was a blessed and useful life, but very wearying; and we can fancy how trying it must have been for Mrs. Booth after her marriage not to have any home of her own, but to billet first in one stranger's house, and then in another's.

But she did not complain, though we see what it cost her by a letter she writes to her mother, telling the good news that they are to live in lodgings while at Sheffield :—

'You cannot think,' she writes, 'with what joy I look forward to being to ourselves once more. For though I get literally oppressed with kindness, I must say I would prefer a home where we could sit down together at our own little table, myself the mistress, and my husband the only guest. But the work of God so abundantly prospers that I dare not repine, or else I feel this constant packing and unpacking and staying amongst strangers to be a great burden, especially while so weak and poorly. But then I have many mercies and advantages. My precious William is all I desire, and without this what would the most splendid home be but a glittering bauble?'

For several years Mrs. Booth travelled in this way from place to place, helping, cheering, and encouraging her husband in his soul-saving campaigns. She felt her duty lay here, and even when she had a little son to care for, she was unwilling to settle down. Writing to her mother, who urged her to leave off this trying life; or, at any rate, to hand the baby over to her, she says :—

'My objection to leaving William gets stronger as I see the need he has of my presence, care, and sympathy; neither is he willing for it himself. Nor can I make up my mind to parting with Willie.'

Mrs. Booth's object was to be a help to her husband—not a hindrance; to push him forward in his soul-saving work—not to hold him back; and therefore, instead of rejoicing, as most wives and mothers would have done, when a settled home and work were offered him, she was doubtful.

'Personally considered,' she writes to her mother, 'I care nothing about it. I feel that a good rest in one place will be a boon to us. Anyhow, if God wills him to be an Evangelist, He will open the way. I find that I love the work itself far more than I thought I did, and I am willing to risk something for it.'

After this came several years of great conflict and struggle. The Conference (or, as we would say, Headquarters) under whom The General worked did not wish him to continue the great Salvation Campaigns for which God had so marvellously fitted him. They wanted him to 'settle down,' and spend perhaps several years in one place like ordinary ministers.

To please those who were over him he

did this, and spent four years in one town. But though God blessed his efforts, The General was convinced that he was called to greater things. He loved the sinners; wherever he went crowds flocked to hear him, and the vilest were converted. Was it God's will, therefore, that he should sacrifice the work his soul loved, and 'settle down' into an ordinary life, helping and reaching only the people of one small city?

This question our Army Mother helped him to decide. Try to picture her position. She had by this time a family of little children, and her health was very delicate. By counselling The General to 'settle down,' as his friends wished him to do, she would have a nice home, a comfortable income, and, above all, the constant presence of her husband, who would no longer need to leave her on his long soul-saving tours.

By refusing the position offered, and choosing instead to take up the 'evangelistic life' again, The General turned his back on salary, home, and work, and went out into the world, with his wife and four children, friendless and alone. Do you wonder that the struggle was a severe one?

'Pray for me,' she wrote to her mother, when the question was about to be settled. 'I have many a conflict in regard to the proposed new departure; not as to our support—I feel as though I can trust the Lord implicitly for all that; but the Devil tells me I shall never be able to endure the loneliness and separation of the life. He draws many a picture of most dark and melancholy shade. But I cling to the promise, "No man hath forsaken," etc., and, having sworn to my own hurt, may I stand fast. I have told William that if he takes the step, and it should bring me to the workhouse, I would never say one upbraiding word. No. To blame him for making such a sacrifice for God and conscience' sake would be worse than wicked. So, whatever be the result, I shall make up my mind to endure it patiently, looking to the Lord for grace and strength.'

But if it was difficult for Mrs. Booth, the path was equally dark and hard for The General.

'William hesitates,' she writes a few weeks later. 'He thinks of me and the children, and I appreciate his love and care. But I tell him that God will provide, if he will only go straight on in the path of duty. It is strange that I, who always used to shrink from the sacrifice, should be the first in making it. But when I made the surrender I did it whole-heartedly, and ever since I have been like another being. Oh, pray for us yet more and more! We have no money coming in from any quarter now. Nor has William any invitations at present. The time is unfavourable. I am much tempted to feel it hard that God has not cleared our path more satisfactorily. But I will not "charge God foolishly." I know that His way is often in the whirlwind, and He rides upon the storm: I will try to possess my soul in patience, and to wait on Him.'

Sometimes you have heard your Officers talking in a Meeting, and telling the people that, if they will but step out in faith, and do right, God will open up the way for them. The example of our General and Army Mother has taught us this lesson, for few ever took a step of faith into greater darkness and difficulty than they did at this time.

'My dearest,' writes Mrs. Booth to her mother, 'is starting for London. Pray for him. He is much harassed. But I have promised to keep a brave heart. At times it appears to me that God may have something very glorious in store for us, and when

He has tried us He will bring us forth as gold. It will not be the first time I have taken a leap in the dark, humanly speaking, for conscience' sake.'

It was, indeed, a ' leap in the dark ': to break up their little home in the North, and, travelling by boat, to save expense, to bring their four children to Mrs. Mumford's house in London. There they separated: the father and mother went to Cornwall, to hold a Salvation campaign in a little chapel that had been lent to them, and the children remained behind.

Of the marvellous way in which God blessed the Cornish work, I cannot stop to tell you. Mrs. Booth's name as a preacher was by this time becoming as widely known as that of her husband; and they went from one place to another, at first together, and then, afterwards, separately, so as to be able to do more good, for four long years.

Whenever possible, our Army Mother took her children with her: she never left them to others when she could help it, and later on I shall tell you what a devoted and tender mother she was; but the strain of those four long years no one will ever know. I want you to see the dark as well as the bright side of her wonderful life; and here is part of a letter to her mother, written at that time:—

'I feel dreadfully unsettled at present. I don't like this mode of living at all. William has now been away from home, except on Friday and Saturday, for twelve weeks. I long to get fixed together again once more. The going backwards and forwards and being in other people's houses does not suit William. Nor do I like leaving home for the Sabbaths. I am much tempted to look gloomily towards the future. But "my heart is fixed." "I will trust, and not be afraid."'

Then again, a little later on:—

'Pray for me. I sometimes feel as though I had taken a path which is too hard for me, and duties too heavy for me to perform; but it is my privilege to say, and to feel, "I can do all things through Christ which strengtheneth me."'

Once again she says:—

'Well, the Lord help us to be faithful to our convictions, even in the dark and cloudy day! I have felt it hard work to do so lately. Many a time have I longed to be where the weary are at rest.

'Well, we must labour and wait a little

longer; it may be that the clouds will break, and surround us with sunshine. Anyway, God lives above the clouds, and He will direct our path.'

The General and Mrs. Booth were holding Salvation services in London when our Army Mother was called to make a fresh sacrifice, never dreaming of the wonderful results that would spring from it. You shall read about it in her own words, spoken many years afterwards:—

'I remember well,' she says, 'when The General decided at last to give up the evangelistic life and to devote himself to the Salvation of the East-Enders. He had come home from a Meeting one night, tired out, as usual. It was between eleven and twelve o'clock. Flinging himself into an easy chair, he said to me, "O Kate, as I passed by the doors of the flaming gin-palaces to-night I seemed to hear a voice sounding in my ears, 'Where can you go and find such heathen as these, and where is there so great a need for your labours?' And I felt as though I ought at every cost to stop and preach to these East-End crowds."

'I remember the emotion that this produced in my soul. I sat gazing into the fire, and the Devil whispered to me, "This means another new departure—another start in life."

'The question of our support I saw at once to be a serious difficulty. Hitherto we had been able to meet our expenses by the collections which we had made from our respectable audiences. But it was impossible to suppose that we could do so among the poverty-stricken East-Enders. We did not then see things as we do to-day. We were afraid even to ask for a collection among the East London crowds.

'Nevertheless, I did not answer discouragingly. After a moment's pause for thought and prayer, I answered, "Well, if you feel you ought to stay, stay. We have trusted the Lord once for our support, and we can trust Him again."'

Mrs. Booth, when she answered like this, had no idea of all that was to follow. She never dreamt that, from The General's standing alone in Whitechapel, a mighty wave of Salvation would sweep over the earth, nor that God was about to raise up an Army of which she and The General were to be the leaders.

But, as always before, she willingly agreed to whatever would be for God's glory and the Salvation of souls; and we all know to-day how, from that little Whitechapel beginning, grew the Christian Mission, and how, at last, the Christian Mission became The Salvation Army.

Do not think, however, that our dear Army Mother's consecration stopped here! No, indeed. One by one, as they became old enough, she gave up her children to the Work, and we shall never know all we owe as an Army to her beautiful spirit of devotion and sacrifice.

Let us stand together by her open grave in the autumn twilight. Her twenty-six years of fight and toil in The Salvation Army are over now, her spirit has been summoned Home. Listen. The Army Founder himself is the speaker. He is recalling the forty years which he and our dear Army Mother had trod together, and his words sum up better than any other words could do what she was to our Leader:—

'If you had had a tree,' he said, speaking to the vast crowd that stood round the grave, 'that had grown up in your garden, under your window, which for forty years had been your shadow from the burning sun, whose flowers had been the adornment and beauty of your life, whose fruit had been almost the stay of your existence, and the gardener had come along and swung his glittering axe and cut it down before your eyes, I think you would feel as though you had a blank—it might not be a big one—but a little blank in your life.

'If you had had a servant who for all this long time had served you without fee or reward, who had administered, for very love, to your health and comfort, and who suddenly passed away, you would miss that servant.

'If you had had a counsellor who, in hours—continually occurring—of perplexity and amazement, had ever advised you, and seldom advised wrong; whose advice you had followed, and seldom had reason to regret it; and the counsellor, while you were in the same intricate mazes of your existence, had passed away, you would miss that counsellor.

'If you had had a friend who had understood your very nature, the rise and fall of your feelings, the bent of your thoughts, and the purpose of your existence; a friend whose communion had ever been pleasant—the most pleasant of all other friends—to whom you had ever turned with satisfaction, and your friend had been taken away, you would feel some sorrow at the loss.

'If you had had a mother for your children who had cradled and nursed and trained them for the service of the living God, in which you most delighted—a mother, indeed, who had never ceased to bear their sorrows on her heart, and who had been ever willing to pour forth that heart's blood in order to nourish them, and that darling mother had been taken from your side, you would feel it a sorrow.

'If you had had a wife, a sweet love of a wife, who for forty years had never given you real cause for grief; a wife who had stood with you, side by side, in the battle's front, who had been a comrade to you, ever willing to interpose herself between you and the enemy, and ever the strongest when the battle was fiercest, and your beloved one had fallen before your eyes, I am sure there would be some excuse for your sorrow.

'Well, my comrades, you can roll all these qualities into one personality, and what would be lost in all I have lost in one. There has been taken away from me the light of my eyes, the inspiration of my soul, and we are about to lay all that remains of her in the grave. I have been looking right at the bottom of it here, and calculating how soon they may bring and lay me alongside of her, and my cry to God has been that every remaining hour of my life may make me readier to come and join her in death, to go and embrace her in life in the Eternal City.'

V

THE SPEAKER

'I will never speak to sinners so that one man or woman in my audience can stand up and say, "You might have warned me more faithfully, spoken more plainly than you did." I would rather die than that should be the case.'—Mrs. Booth.

No one must think that Mrs. Booth became a great speaker all in a moment, or by any 'royal road.' She started when about eighteen, as many a Corps Cadet has since done, by just taking a class or Company on Sundays, never dreaming of doing more. An elder girls' Company was given to her; and she had fifteen girls to teach, whose ages varied from twelve to nineteen.

Two half-days she spent every week in preparing for her Company, and in trying to make each lesson end in a practical way, so as to do them real good.

Then on Sunday, when the rest of the children had been dismissed, Miss Mumford would beg to be given the key of the room and would remain behind, holding a little Prayer Meeting with her girls. Sometimes they would stay on for an hour and a half, and many by this means became truly converted.

Often with so much praying and singing Catherine quite lost her voice before the end of the Meeting; but, so long as souls were saved, she did not mind that.

Soon after her marriage Mrs. Booth took another class of this same kind, and also a little sort of Sergeants' Meeting, and then—for you see our Army Mother was led on, just as you or I may be, step by step—she gave a short talk to the Band of Hope children (something like our Band of Love of to-day) on the evils of drink.

'Oh, how I wish,' she wrote to her father, 'that I had started speaking years ago!'

A little later on Mr. and Mrs. Booth moved to Gateshead, and there the people were very much surprised to hear their minister's wife pray aloud when her husband had done speaking; for in those days very few women thought of praying, much less of speaking, in public.

'Since you can pray so beautifully, will you come and talk to us on our special

Prayer-Meeting night?' some of the people asked. But Mrs. Booth was horrified.

'Of course, I said "No,"' she wrote. 'I don't know what they can be thinking of.'

Just at this time an argument began in one of the newspapers as to whether women had the right to speak for God or not. Mrs. Booth wrote an answer to this question—you can read it for yourself in her book, 'Practical Religion'—and she showed from God's Word, that women have the same right to help to get people saved that the men have. The little pamphlet was already printed and being widely read, and our Army Mother lay alone in her room very ill, when the thought flashed into her soul, 'You have been helping other women to preach and to speak for God. What about yourself?'

'Oh, no, Lord, not me; I can't. I am, as Thou knowest, the most timid and bashful disciple ever saved by grace.' That was her answer.

Then the Lord took her back to the days when she first gave herself to Him, at the age of fifteen. He showed her that all the way along this one thing had hindered and stopped her from 'being the blessing or from getting the blessing He intended.'

'Lord,' she cried, 'if Thou wilt come back to me as in the old days, I will obey, though I die in the attempt.'

But at the moment God seemed not to answer her cry, and when she was well again all went on as before.

Three months later Mrs. Booth was quietly sitting one Sunday morning in chapel with her eldest boy, when a very wonderful thing happened. You shall read about it in her own words:—

'I felt much depressed in mind,' she says, 'and was not expecting anything particular, but as the testimonies proceeded I felt the Holy Spirit come upon me. It seemed as if a voice said to me: "Now, if you were to go and testify, you know I would bless it to your own soul as well as to the people!" I gasped again, and said in my heart: "Yes, Lord, I believe Thou wouldst, but I cannot do it!" I had forgotten my vow.

'A moment afterwards there flashed across my mind the memory of the time when I had promised the Lord that I would obey Him at all costs. And then the voice seemed to ask me if this was consistent with that promise. I almost jumped up and said, "No, Lord, it is the old thing over again. But I cannot do it!" I felt as though I would sooner die than speak. And then the Devil said, " Besides, you are not prepared. You will look like a fool, and will have nothing to say." He made a mistake. He over-reached himself for once. It was this word that settled it. " Ah!" I said, " this is just the point. I have never yet been willing to be a fool for Christ. Now I will be one!"

'Without stopping another moment, I rose up from my seat and walked down the aisle. My dear husband thought something had happened to me, and so did the people. We had been there two years, and they knew my timid, bashful nature. He stepped down, and asked me, " What is the matter, my dear?" I replied, " I want to say a word!" He was so taken by surprise that he could only say, " My dear wife wishes to speak!" and sat down. For years he had been trying to persuade me to do it. Only that very week he had wanted me to go and address a little Cottage Meeting of some twenty working people, but I had refused.

'I stood—God only knows how—and if any mortal ever did hang on the arm of Omnipotence, I did. I just stood and told the people how it had come about. I confessed, as I think everybody should who has been in the wrong and has misrepresented the religion of Jesus Christ. I said, " I dare say many of you have been looking upon me as a very devoted woman, and one who has been living faithfully to God. But I have come to realize that I have been disobeying Him, and thus brought darkness and leanness into my soul. I have promised the Lord to do so no longer, and have come to tell you that henceforth I will be obedient to the holy vision."

'There was more weeping, they said, in the chapel that day than on any previous occasion. Many dated a renewal in righteousness from that very moment, and began a life of devotion and consecration to God.

'Now I might have "talked good" to them till now. That honest confession did what twenty years of preaching could not have accomplished.'

After this wonderful victory Mrs. Booth never again drew back. The same night she spoke once more, with even greater power than in the morning, and before long invitations came pouring in from all parts, for wherever she went souls were saved and people sanctified.

But it cost her a great deal to preach like this. She writes of one Meeting held soon after:—

'I got on very well, and had three beautiful cases, but I cannot tell you how I felt all day about it. I could neither eat nor sleep. I never was in such a state, and when I saw the people, I felt like melting away. However, I got through.'

Even to the last, when she was known all round the world as one of the greatest women-preachers of the day, she never spoke without feeling deeply the responsibility and importance of her work, nor without having prepared carefully beforehand what she wanted to say.

It was very difficult for her, with four little children, the eldest only four years and three months old, to get enough time and quiet. We should have said it was impossible, for she was not well off, and could not afford to put her sewing out, or to have many servants to work for her; but she says:—

'God forced me to begin to think and work, and He gave me grace and strength to do it. Many a time while I was nursing my baby I was thinking of what I should say next Sunday, and between times I noted down with a pencil the thoughts as they struck me. Then I would appear with an outline scratched in pencil, trusting in the Lord to give me the power of His Holy Spirit; and from the day I began He has never allowed me to open my mouth without giving me signs of His presence and blessing.'

The two books she always used in getting ready for her Meetings were her Bible and Concordance.

In later years she taught her children how to prepare for their Meetings, and some of the advice she gives is very helpful to Corps Cadets.

' "Jesus wept," ' she writes to her eldest girl, who was then fourteen, ' would be a nice subject for you at one of your little Meetings. And you could find some texts to show how David wept, and Daniel, and Jeremiah, etc., if you like it. But don't take it because *I* say so—you must ask the Lord for your subjects.'

Later on, however, as The Salvation Army grew, Mrs. Booth felt that, though it was just as necessary to prepare, yet to speak from notes was often not helpful to either the Officer or the people, so she writes to one of her sons:—

'Get out of them! They don't fit our work. When you get on, you don't want them; and when you don't, they are no good. At first, if your memory won't serve you, just jot on a small bit of paper the size of a ticket your main divisions in large writing, but no more. Like this:—

‘ Day of wrath is come.
‘ 1. God’s wrath.
‘ 2. Just wrath.
‘ 3. Uttermost wrath.
‘ 4. Eternal wrath.’

On the platform Mrs. Booth’s manner was as simple and natural as when by her own fireside; anything ‘ put on ’ or affected she hated.

‘ If I were asked,’ she says, ‘ to put into one word what I consider to be the greatest hindrance to the success of Divine truth, even when spoken by sincere and real people, I should say *stiffness*. Simplicity is indispensable to success, *naturalness* in putting the truth. It seems as if people, the moment they come to religion, put on a different tone, a different look and manner—in short, become unnatural.’

But Mrs. Booth not only prepared for her Meetings by thought and study, but she prepared most of all by prayer.

‘ Oh, if we could,’ she writes, ‘ get more of the spirit of prayer into those who love God! Few understand it at all.

‘ I always find an exact proportion in the

results to the spirit of intercession I have had beforehand. That is why I like to be alone in lodgings.'

Before her Meeting she would wrestle and plead with God for hours, in tears and agony, and then would face her congregation overflowing with love and faith.

'Pray for me,' she writes during her marvellous Portsmouth campaign. 'No one knows how I feel. I think I never realized my responsibility as I did on Sunday night. I felt really awful before rising to speak. The sight almost overwhelmed me. With its two galleries, its dome-like roof and vast proportions, when crammed with people, the building presents a most imposing appearance. The top gallery is ten or twelve seats deep in front, and it was full of men. Such a sight as I have never seen on any previous occasion. Oh, how I *yearned* over them! I felt as if it would be a small thing to die *there and then*, if that would have brought them to Jesus.'

Nothing short of men and women getting converted satisfied her.

'They say,' she writes of another campaign, 'the sinners here will "*bide some bringing down*." Well, the Lord can do it. They tell me, too, that I am immensely popular with the people. But *that* is no comfort unless they will be saved.'

She laboured to get the truth home to the hearts of her listeners, and that is why her talking was so blessed.

'God made you responsible,' she said, 'not for delivering the truth, but for GETTING IT IN—getting it home, fixing it in the conscience as a red-hot iron, as a bolt, straight from His throne; and He has given you also the *power to do it;* and if you do not do it, *blood* will be on your skirts. Oh, this genteel way of putting the truth! How God hates it! "If you please, dear friends, will you listen? If you please, will you be converted? Will you come to Jesus? Shall we read just this, that, and the other?" No more like apostolic preaching than darkness is like light.'

How can I show you some of the marvellous results of her preaching? In every part of our land her influence and words made themselves felt; the largest buildings were crowded with all classes of society, and glorious cases of conversion and sanctification crowned her labours everywhere. A lady who was at some of her women's

Meetings at Lye, near Birmingham, tells us:—

'The women left their work, and in all sorts of odd costumes flocked to the Meetings, some with bonnets, some with shawls fastened over their head, others with little children clinging to their necks. All, with eager, inquiring faces, took their seats and listened to the gracious words which fell from the lips of dear Mrs. Booth. And when the invitation was given, what a scene ensued! It baffles all description. Crowding, weeping, rushing to the penitent-form came convicted sinners and repentant backsliders. When the form was filled the penitents dropped upon their knees in the aisles or in their seats, so that it was difficult to move about.'

When holding some Meetings in a Rotherhithe chapel (for The Army was only just beginning its work, and our Army Mother took Meetings in different churches and chapels up and down the land), the victories were just as glorious, and one of her Converts says:—

'There were many remarkable cases of conversion at these Meetings. Amongst others there were the two daughters of a publican. When one sister was saved the other went to hear Mrs. Booth on purpose to ridicule the services. But she was seized with such an agonizing realization of her sins that she came down from the top of the gallery to the penitent-form, crying out aloud, "I must come! I must come!" Soon after their father gave up the public-house, and they afterwards became members of Mr. Spurgeon's Tabernacle.

'I have seen as many as thirty persons seeking Salvation in a single Meeting, and some years afterwards, when I looked at the register of our chapel, I found about one hundred names of those who had professed to be converted at this time.'

Our Army Mother, too, was equally straight and fearless with the rich when, later on, they also came in crowds to hear her. She had but one message and one gospel for all alike. She says, 'By God's help I will not regard the person of man, but will plainly and fearlessly declare the truth, come what may.' God honoured this spirit, and her Meetings in the West-End of London, where the great and rich live, were some of the most glorious of her life. Of one such she writes:—

'The Lord has very graciously stood by me, and given me much precious fruit. Last

Sunday we had the Hall crowded, and a large proportion of gentlemen. The Lord was there in power, and twenty-one came forward—some for Salvation and some for purity. Several were most blessed cases of full surrender. We did not get away till nearly six, and we began at three. Everybody is amazed at this for the West-End! The audience is very select, we never having published a bill. Pray much, dear friend, that God may do a deep and permanent work in this Babylon. It seems as though He gave me words of fire for them, and they sat spellbound.'

You say you wish you had heard her speak? Indeed, we all wish you had: you could never have forgotten it. But several of her addresses were taken down in shorthand at the time, and are reprinted in her books, so you can get and read them; and they will bless and teach you as they have taught thousands before you.

VI

THE MOTHER

'A lady once said to me, "How have you managed to get your children converted so early?" "Oh," I said, "I have been beforehand with the Devil." '—MRS. BOOTH.

I HAVE already told you how Mrs. Booth had the true mother spirit when but a little child, loving and tending her dolls as if they had been real babies; you will, therefore, guess that with her own children she was the best and most careful of mothers. She began early to train them in the right way, and never left them unless forced to do so.

'I cannot part with Willie,' she writes to her mother, who offered to free Mrs. Booth by taking charge of the baby for her; 'first, because I know the child's affections could not but be weaned from us; and secondly, because the next year will be the most important of his life with reference to managing his will; and in this I cannot but distrust you. I know, my darling mother, you could not wage war with his self-will so resolutely as to subdue it. And then my child would be ruined, for he must be taught implicit, uncompromising obedience.'

But long before writing this she had already claimed her boy for God and His war. 'I had from the first,' she says, 'definite longings over Bramwell, and lifted him up to God as soon as I had strength to do so, especially desiring he should be a teacher of Holiness.'

These prayers began to be answered very early. The boy had a truthful and conscientious nature. Never, his mother says, does she remember his telling her a lie. But, for all that, he needed, as do all children, training and teaching, and Mrs. Booth was too wise not to be firm. She writes therefore:—

'I believe he will be a thoroughly noble lad, if I can preserve him from all evil influence. The Lord help me! I have had to whip him twice lately severely for disobedience, and it has cost me some tears. But it has done him good, and I am reaping the reward already of my self-sacrifice. The Lord help me to be faithful and firm as a rock in the path of duty towards my children!'

We know how practical our Army Mother always was; sentimental pity without help she despised. When her little son, therefore, saw and pitied a small boy with shoeless feet, his mother quickly reminded him of his little money-box.

'Would you rather keep the money for barley-sugar, Willie, or give it to the poor boy?' she asked. 'Give it to the boy,' he said at once, and so learnt his first lesson in self-denial.

When the boy was seven years old he was converted, to his mother's deepest joy. Some time before she had talked to him in a Meeting, and urged him to get saved. The boy sat still and said nothing. 'Willie, I insist,' said his mother at last. 'You must answer me. Will you give your heart to God or not? Yes or no?'

Willie looked up in her face steadily and answered back 'No.'

Mrs. Booth said no more just then, but held on in faith and prayer, and some months later, to her unutterable thankfulness, she found him squeezed in among a number of other children at the penitent-form. He had, unasked, made his way there, and was weeping and confessing his sins with all his heart.

Needless to say, he was faithfully dealt with, and the boy, now our beloved General, dates his conversion from that moment. A little later Mrs. Booth wrote of him:—

> ‘ Willie has begun to serve God, of course as a child, but still, I trust, taught of the Spirit. I feel a great increase of responsibility with respect to him. Oh! to cherish the tender plant of grace aright. Lord help!’

And as with the eldest so with the other seven. One by one they gave their hearts to the Lord as soon as they grew old enough to do so.

‘ She used to gather us round her,’ says one of her daughters, ‘ and pray with us. I wore then a low frock, and her hot tears would often drop upon my neck, sending a thrill through me which I can never forget.’

She would pray again and again that she might lay them in their graves rather than she should see them grow up wicked.

Mrs. Booth was very particular about the way in which her children were dressed.

Of course, there was no uniform in those days, but The Army spirit was already in The Army Mother, and she would not have any finery or show, either for herself or her children.

'Accept,' she writes to her mother, 'my warm thanks for the little frock you sent. There is only one difficulty—it is too smart. We must set an example in this direction. I feel no temptation now to decorate myself, but I cannot say the same about the children; and yet, Oh, I see I must be decided. Besides, I find it would be dangerous for their own sakes. The seed of vanity is too deeply sown in their young hearts for me to dare to cultivate it.'

Even in her early days Mrs. Booth felt how wrong it was to spend time and money over dress:—

'I remember feeling condemned,' she says, 'when quite a child, not more than eight years old, at having to wear a lace tippet such as was fashionable in those days. From a worldly point of view it would have been considered, no doubt, very neat and consistent. But on several occasions I had good crying fits over it. Not only did I instinctively feel it to be immodest, because people could see through it, but I thought it was not such as a Christian child should wear.'

In everything to do with her home Mrs. Booth was a most practical and careful mother. She hated waste and luxury, but her children were always properly dressed and fed and cared for, and never lacked what was necessary for them.

Ladies who had been blessed by her words came to consult her about their souls, and to their surprise found the great preacher, not shut away in her study, but hard at work perhaps ironing the baby's pinafores, or cutting out a pair of trousers for one of her boys! 'I must try,' she said, when she began to live this two-fold life, 'to do all in the kitchen as well as in the pulpit to the glory of God. The Lord help me.' He did help her, and it was this practical mother-spirit at home which gave her so much force and power on the platform.

As the children grew older, they were more away from her side, and her letters to them are suitable, not only to her actual sons and daughters, but to her spiritual grandchildren who will read this little book. Therefore I am going to give you some extracts, which you may take as though written by our Army Mother straight to your own heart.

To one of her boys at school she wrote :—

'I do hope you are industrious, and do not lose time in play and inattention. Remember Satan steals his marches on us by *littles*—a minute now, and a minute then. Be on the look out, and don't be cheated by him!

'All your little trials will soon be over, so far as school life is concerned; and every one of them, if borne with patience, will make you a wiser and better man. Never forget my advice about not listening to *secrets!* Don't hear anything that needs to be whispered—it is sure to be bad. Choose the boys to be your companions who most love and fear God, and pray together when you can, and help each other.'

Here is a very beautiful letter written when one of her children desired to go in for some higher education, which Mrs. Booth feared might spoil the soul life :—

'I do so want you and all my children to live supremely for God. I do so deeply deplore my own failure compared with what my life might have been, and I feel as if I could die to save you from making a mistake. Perhaps you say, "You don't want me, then, to learn any more?" Yes, I do, a great deal more; but of the right kind, in the right way, and for a right purpose, even the *highest good of your race.* I would like you to learn to put your thoughts together well, to think logically and clearly, to speak powerfully—that is, with good but simple language—and to write clearly and well.'

Just the wish we have now for all our Young People!

Early in their childhood the elder children were taught to be responsible for the younger, and when at school they were given places of trust as monitors, and so on. As if knowing the responsibilities they would by and by be called to fill in our ranks, Mrs. Booth gives them some wise counsel:—

'I hope,' she says to one who has been left in charge of the other children, 'you will show yourself to be a true son of your mother, and a consistent disciple of the Lord. Very much depends on you as to the ease and comfort of managing the little ones. Do all you can. Be forbearing where only your own feelings or comfort are concerned, and don't raise unnecessary difficulties; but where their obedience to us or their health is at stake, be firm in trying to put them right.'

'I am pleased,' she says to one of the boys who has been in charge of others at school, 'that Mr. W. puts such confidence in you; but do not be puffed up by it. Remember how weak you are, and ask the Lord to save you from conceit and self-sufficiency. Try to be fair and just in all dealings with the boys—i.e. do not be hard on a boy whom you may not happen to like so well as another; but be fair, and treat all alike when left in charge.'

Again, she warns one of them against extremes, even in well doing:—

'You are under a mistake to suppose that sacrificing your recreation-time will help you in the end. It will not. Cramming the mind acts just in the same way as cramming the stomach. It is what you digest well that benefits you, not what you cram in. So many hours spent in study, and then relaxation and walking, will do your mind much more good than "all work, and no play." Now mark this. Do not be looking so much at what you *have* to do as to what you are *doing*. Leave the future (you may spend it in Heaven), and go steadily on doing to-day's work in to-day's hours, with recreation in between to shake the seed in. One step well and firmly taken is better than two with a slip backwards. Poor human nature seems as though it must go to extremes—either all or none, too much or too little, idleness or being killed with work! May the Lord show you the happy medium.'

'I was sorry about the cause of the accident. I don't like that way of doing things in fun! Though it was very wrong and wicked of the boy to throw the brick, yet it would have been better to let him look at the guinea-pigs being fed, and thus have pleased him. There was no harm in what he wanted to do. You should watch against a hectoring spirit, and mind the difference between a sacrifice of truth and principle, and one only of self-importance or of mere feeling. If a boy wants you to do wrong, then be firm as a rock and brave for God and goodness.'

'Mind your soul,' she says at another time. 'Do not let your thoughts get so absorbed, even in study, as to lead you to forget your Bible and to neglect prayer.'

Later, again, as a wise mother she warns them in the tenderest way against their special temptations.

Against lightness:—

'Be watchful against levity. C. is a good, devoted fellow, but naturally an incorrigible joker. It may not hurt him much, because it is his nature; but it will hurt you if you give way to it. It hurts nearly everybody.

Watch! Don't descend to buffoonery. While you become all things to win some, don't forfeit your natural self-respect and the dignity of your position as a servant of Christ.'

Against too much talk:—

'The Spirit is teaching you this—is showing you that you must be more silent. The tongue is one of the greatest enemies to grace (James iii. 5-13). Strive to obey these teachings of God. Yield yourself up to obey; and though you sometimes fail and slip, do not be discouraged, but yield yourself up again and again, and plead more fervently with God to keep you. Fourteen years ago you were learning to walk, and in the process you got many a tumble. But now you can not only walk yourself, but teach others. So, spiritually, if you will only let God lead you, He will perfect that which is lacking in you.'

But it was not at first easy for the mother-spirit in Mrs. Booth to allow her delicate girls of fourteen or fifteen to undertake a public life, and to speak and sing at the street corners, surrounded by a rough, low crowd. Such a thing was unheard-of in those days.

Once, hearing that her daughter Catherine had spoken in the open air to a large crowd, Mrs. Booth objected, as other mothers have since objected: the girl was too young as yet—she must wait awhile.

But her eldest son, looking at his mother in the tenderest and most solemn way, said, 'Mamma, dear, you will have to settle this question with God; for Katie is as surely called and inspired by Him for the particular work as you are yourself.'

Mrs. Booth said no more. She took this as the voice of God, and gave her girl up to the marvellous work which God had called her to do.

Later she writes of her to a friend:—

'Join me in praying that she may be kept humble and simple, and that all that the Lord has given her may be used for Him.'

'I see,' she says, writing at this same time to her daughter, 'what a glorious, blessed, useful life you may live; but I also see your danger, and I pray for you that you may be enabled to cast aside the world in every form, to look down upon its opinions, and to despise its spirit, maxims, and fashions.'

Later on, again, came the days when the boys had to choose, as you have to do, how they would spend their lives. Mrs. Booth might be writing to a Corps Cadet of to-day when, in a letter to one of her sons, she says:—

'I hope the Lord will make you so miserable everywhere and at everything else that you will be *compelled* to preach! Oh, my boy, the Lord wants such as you—*just such*—to go out amongst the people, seeking nothing but the things that are Jesus Christ's! You are free to do it; able by His grace; born to do it, with splendid opportunities. Will you not rise to your destiny? "Have courage, and be strong, and I (the I Am) will be with thee." "Get thee out, and I will go with thee." Dare you not take hold of the arm that holds the world and all things up? And if you do, can you fail? The Lord gird you with His strength, and make your brow brass, and your tongue as a flame of fire. You *must preach!*'

To another of her boys she writes:—

'You may, perhaps, be wanted to stand and do battle for the Lord. Surely you will not sell your birthright? The Lord help you! Take hold of David's God. Hold your head up, keep your shoulders back, and go forward.'

Again:—

'This is what the world wants: men of one idea—that of getting people saved. There are plenty of men of one idea—that of *gold*-getting. They make no secret of it; they are of a worldly spirit. Now we want men who are set on soul-saving, who are not ashamed to let everybody know it—men of a Christ-like spirit. There need be no mistake or mystery about it. "By their fruits ye shall know them." Paul and every other man of like spirit has had his fruits, and will have to the end of time. It is "Not by might, nor by power, but by *My Spirit*, saith the Lord of Hosts." '

With one of her daughters she reasons and pleads:—

'Oh, it seems to me that if I were in your place—young, no cares or anxieties, with such a start, such influence, and such a prospect—I should not be able to contain myself for joy! I should, indeed, aspire to be the "bride of the Lamb," and to follow Him in conflict for the Salvation of poor, lost, miserable man. I pray the Lord to show it to you, and so to enamour you of Himself, that you may see and feel it to be your chief joy to win them for Him. I say I pray for this—yes, I groan for it, with groanings that cannot be uttered; and if ever you tell me it is so, I shall be overjoyed.

'I don't want you to make any vows (unless, indeed, the Spirit leads you to do so); but I want you to set your mind and heart on winning souls, and to leave everything else with the Lord. When you do this you will be happy—Oh, so happy! Your soul will then find perfect rest. The Lord grant it to you, my dear child.'

She made all her children feel that the only reward they could give her for her ceaseless toil and labour on their behalf was that they should give themselves to the War:—

'I hope, my dear boy, that, whatever sense of obligation or gratitude you have towards me, you will try to return it by resolutely resisting all temptation to evil, and by fitting yourself to your utmost to be useful to your fellow-men. I ask from you, as I asked from God, no other reward. If I know my own heart, I would rather that you should work for the Salvation of souls, making bad hearts good, and miserable homes happy, and preparing joy and gladness for men at the Judgment bar, if you only get bread and cheese all your life, than that you should fill any other capacity with £10,000 per year.'

To one of her children, when tempted to be over-anxious, she writes:—

'Keep your mind quiet. Lean back on God, and don't worry. It is His affair, and if you have done what you could, that is enough. Alas! how little we have of the faith that can "stand still, and see the Salvation of God." What would you do if you were put in custody for two years, like Paul was? And yet that imprisonment at Rome sent the Gospel far and wide! God's ways are not our ways. He takes in the whole field at once, and does the best He can for the entire world. Human wisdom never has been able at the time to comprehend His plans, but years after it has often seen their wisdom. Let us learn to trust in the dark—to stand still.'

To another, tried and discouraged at the start of his public life:—

'I have only a minute or two; but, lest you should think I don't sympathize with you, I send you a line. You ask, did I ever feel so? Yes, I think just as bad as any mortal *could* feel—*empty*, inside and out, as though I had nothing human or Divine to aid me, as if all Hell were let loose upon me.

But I have generally felt *the worse before the best results*, which proves it was Satanic opposition. And it has been the same with many of God's most honoured instruments. I believe nearly all who are truly called of God to special usefulness pass through this buffeting.

'It stands to sense, if there is a Devil, that he should desperately withstand those whom he sees are going to be used of God. Supposing *you* were the Devil, and had set your heart on circumventing God, how would you do it but by opposing those who were bent on building up His Kingdom? He hopes to drive us from the field by blood and fire and vapour of smoke. But our Captain fought and won the battle for us, and we have only to hold on long enough, and victory is sure. "Courage!" your Captain cries. "Only be thou strong, and of good courage, and I will be with thee, and teach thee what to say."

'"He hath chosen the weak things." He has not *made shift with them*—taken them because there were no others. No! He hath *chosen* them. Will He ever forsake them, and thus make Himself a laughing-stock for Hell? Never! Will He ever let the Devil say, "Ah, ah! He chose this weak one, and then let him fail"? No, no, no!'

On the important question of courtship, she writes :—

'The Devil sets such innocent-looking traps—*spiritual* traps—to catch young people! Ah, he is a serpent still! Beware of his devices, and always cry to God for wisdom and strength of will to put down all foolish tampering. You are born for greater things. God may want you to be a leader in some vast continent, and you will want a companion and a counsellor—a "helpmeet." The original word means "*a help corresponding to his dignity*." This is the meaning given by the best expositors. Oh, what wisdom there is even in the *words* which God has chosen to express His ideas! "Corresponding to his dignity!" Yes, and no man ever takes one below this mark who does not suffer for it; and, worse still, generations yet unborn have to suffer also. Mind what God says, and keep yourself till that one comes.

'A wrong step on this point, and you are undone. Oh, the misery of an unsuitable match! It is beyond description. I could tell you tales of woe that are now being enacted. But I must wait till we meet.

'I have seen too much of life, and know too much of human nature, to have much confidence in promises given under such circumstances. For my own part, I made up my mind when I was but sixteen that I would not have a man, though a Christian, who should offer to become even an abstainer for my sake. I felt that such a promise would not afford me ground for confidence afterwards. And do not we see enough all round us to show that unless people adopt things on principle, because they see it to be right, they soon change? Look at the folks who promise to give up tobacco and dress, for the sake of getting into berths; how soon it evaporates! No, my lad, wait a bit. "Couldst thou not watch with Me one hour?" Jesus lived a single life for your sake all the way through. Can you not live so till He finds you one after His own heart? I feel sure He will. Pray about it in faith. I am doing so; and God will answer. But Oh, don't run before Him! Wait on the Lord.

'A little longer and you will be saying, "Oh, how glad I am I waited! I have now found a treasure indeed!" When God's time and person are come, He will bring you together. How delighted and satisfied Isaac must have felt when the servant told him the way God led him (Genesis xxiv.).'

When standing by her grave The General said she was *The Army Mother.* He said the truth.

One of her early promises, given to her as a girl, when she only saw its greatness and hid it away in her heart as too sacred to be spoken of, and almost too wonderful ever to be accomplished, were the words: 'I will make thee a mother of nations.'

When called to send her children abroad, she paid to the full the heavy price; but she also saw the glorious outcome, and from her death-bed sent tenderest messages to those of distant lands and far-off nations who owned her as their Army Mother.

VII

THE WORKER

'What the Lord wants is, that you shall go about the business to which He sets you, not asking for an easy post, nor grumbling at a hard one.'—Mrs. Booth.

If she had not been a worker, our Army Mother would have done little with her life. The wonderful call which came to her, her great gifts, the zeal and love which filled her heart, would all have been useless had she not been willing to work, and to work hard, and to work every day.

Stop and think about this. No life accomplishes anything unless it is full of hard work—often work accompanied by much drudgery, whether it is the life of a king or of a poor man. Mrs. Booth has set us all an example in this, for she would work ceaselessly with head or hands or heart, as long as ever her health allowed her to do so. Laziness and idleness of all kinds she detested; nor could she tolerate a lazy person in her service.

She worked first of all in her home. When she spent a morning in her kitchen, the work there was perfectly done. The dinner was ready at the right time, properly cooked, good and wholesome. She allowed no waste and no extravagance. Her bread was light and beautifully baked, and when she had finished her morning's work her kitchen was as neat as when she began. She finished everything, and put it straight as she went along.

It was the same with the children. She was alike nurse and doctor, dressmaker and tailor; she made and mended, washed and ironed for her boys and girls during their early years, and herself attended to every smallest detail of their lives. Strangers who asked where Mrs. Booth bought her children's things, so that they could go to the same shop, could scarcely believe the reply: 'Mamma makes all our clothes herself'—so beautifully were they cut and finished.

And when the little garments were of no further service to her, she would alter and mend them once again, and give them away.

Her baby-clothes, when the last daughter had outgrown them, were given to a member of the Mission for his child.

He will never forget taking the little bundle home to his wife and turning over the tiny things. 'I had often heard Mrs. Booth preach,' he said, 'but those baby-clothes preached a louder sermon to me and my wife than ever her words had done. They were all darned and mended and patched, and the work—but, there, I never saw such stitches! And as we looked, and knew the hours of toil she must have put into them, rather than throw them away, as many another would have done—well, I tell you I listened to her next sermon as I had never listened before.'

And this same diligent, tireless spirit was with her to the last. When on her death-bed, able only to use her left hand, and propped up by pillows, she devised a little frame on which, painfully, stitch by stitch, she could work a last token of love for The General.

When her hands were folded still in death, I saw those slippers. They were beautifully embroidered, one with the words, 'He will keep the feet of His Saints'; and the other with the sure and certain hope which lay beyond the parting, 'Our feet shall stand within thy gates, O Jerusalem'—a fitting and sacred service with which to close her many years of toil and labour for others.

But our Army Mother had another way of working in her home—that is, she worked over others. If a girl wished to learn, Mrs. Booth would take endless trouble in showing her the best way to wash or iron, or clean a grate, or do whatever the work on hand might be. She instructed her servants, explaining to them the reason for doing their duties in a certain way, teaching them forethought and common sense, and dealing faithfully with them over all their failures.

'Better,' she said, in one of her addresses—and she lived it out in her own home—'better take a girl whom you have to teach how to wash a child's face, or to stitch a button on, if she is true and sincere, than have one ever so clever, who will teach your children to lie and deceive.'

She worked, too, over the cases of need and poverty which were often at her door. Not content, like so many, with giving a few coppers to a beggar, or some broken food, she would inquire into the *cause* of the distress; and then, if the need seemed genuine, she would help, either by getting the father work, or by having the home visited and suitable relief given after the true condition of things had been found out.

And this was only a little of the home-work with which her hands were ever full. Of her ceaseless care over her children's mind and soul training I have told you elsewhere. But of her public work perhaps the most exhausting was that which resulted from her Meetings. For she could not rest content with the most careful preparation beforehand, nor with pouring out her whole soul upon the people during the forty or fifty minutes that her address lasted. At the close of the Meeting, whenever her health allowed it, she would labour and toil, often for two hours and more, dealing herself with the penitents, meeting their difficulties, one by one, and was unwilling to leave them until, as far as possible, all had claimed and received the blessing they sought.

The next day, too, she would follow up any special case with a long personal letter from her own pen, or she would arrange another interview, or in some way keep in close, actual touch with the struggling soul, until the step of obedience had been taken, and he or she was fairly started on the Narrow Way.

And it was this careful, earnest, patient after-work which gave such glorious harvests to her soul-saving campaigns. Labour and trouble were a joy to her, if she could but help one sincere, seeking soul into the light.

But remember this: while she so toiled over all who came to her for advice and guidance, she never repeated nor passed on to others their confidences. If she had done so, people would soon have left off coming to her; they would have said, 'We cannot trust her.' She was, as you know, a mighty speaker; but about other people's affairs she was entirely silent—as you must learn to be if you wish to be of any service to God or man.

And Mrs. Booth strove constantly to teach all who were around her to work as she did. 'You have begun well enough—now carry it through,' she would say again and again to her children, and whether it was a doll's frock, or an article for 'The War Cry,' or a series of Meetings, it was always the same. Unfinished, half-done work she detested with all her soul. 'If a thing is worth beginning at all, then it is worth finishing,' she would say; and this great principle followed her through her life in small things as in great.

This was the reason that, on her death-bed, she could say, turning to the Chief of the Staff, 'I have no vain regrets about the past. As far as my strength allowed, I have finished the work I had to do as I went along; and now I leave it, all imperfect as it has been, in His hands.'

Perhaps, by nature, you are not a worker. But what you are not by nature, you can become by grace. God can teach you to love work. And as you work, you will, like our dear Army Mother, learn better and better how to work; and your life, whenever God calls you to lay it down, shall be like hers, not unfinished, but complete.

VIII

GOODNESS

'I see more than ever that the religion which is pleasing to God consists in doing and enduring His will, rather than in good sentiments and feelings. The Lord help us to endure as seeing Him who is invisible.'—MRS. BOOTH.

WHEN our first General stood on that October evening by the grave of his beloved wife, and spoke to us with a breaking heart of our Army Mother, he unfolded to us the three great qualities which made her character so beautiful. First, and foremost, she was good; secondly, she was love; and, thirdly, she was a Warrior. Let us, following The General's outline, look at these three leading qualities in her life. 'First,' he said, 'she was *good*. She was washed in the Blood of the Lamb. To the last moment her cry was "a sinner saved by grace." She was a thorough hater of shams, hypocrisies, and make-believes. Her goodness was of a practical sort. "By their fruits ye shall know them" was a text she often quoted, and one by which she was always willing to be judged.'

It is of this 'goodness of a practical sort' that I want first to tell you, before we consider that soul goodness which made her life so holy.

Mrs. Booth could not imagine any goodness apart from industry. As we have already seen, she considered it a sin to waste precious time. Any one who was lazy she could not endure, and when one such offered for the work she wrote of him:—

'I do hope you will not throw a lot of money away in trying H——, just for want of courage to tell him at once that he will not do, because I am sure that it will be thrown away. It is the *nature* of the man that is at fault, and not his *circumstances*. He is a *drone*, and nothing, no change of place or position, can ever make him into a bee. He never ought to have left his trade; he never *would* have done so if he had thought soul-saving was harder work!'

Extravagance and waste of every kind she abhorred, and had she not been so careful in planning and arranging, her time and money would again and again have run short. The sewing, mending, and housekeeping needed for a family of little children when means are scarce would have been burden enough for most mothers. But besides this came her own letter-writing, preparing for her Meetings, and also the hours she spent consulting and advising The General, whose voice, 'Here, Kate,' would call her from the nursery or kitchen to help him decide some important question.

Again, it was impossible to talk to Mrs. Booth, even for five minutes, without finding how true and sincere she was. To please no one would she keep back the truth, or appear different from her real self.

'I believe,' she writes, when quite a young woman, 'honesty to be the best policy, and I shall act upon it. Let me have truth, if it shakes the foundation of the earth.'

She was sincere and faithful in every part of her nature: faithful with her own soul and in dealing with the souls of others. Great or small, rich or poor, she made no difference, and never held back from reproving sin when it was needful.

'I see more than ever,' she said, 'the need of making righteous people true in their *inward parts.* Let us be more thorough than ever with souls under conviction. Let us not be afraid to wound too deeply. Thousands of professors have never been truly convinced of sin, much less truly converted. Sin to them is *being found out!*'

Though all through her life our Army Mother hungered and thirsted to know God better, and to serve Him more perfectly, yet it was not till some time after her marriage that she received the blessing of a clean heart.

Of the struggle and conflict which she went through, before the blessing of Holiness became hers, she shall tell you in her own words:—

'I had been earnestly seeking all the week to know Jesus as an all-sufficient Saviour dwelling in my heart, and thus cleansing it every moment of all sin; but on Thursday and Friday I laid aside almost everything else, and spent the chief part of the day in reading and prayer, and trying to believe for it. On Thursday afternoon at tea-time I was well-nigh discouraged, and felt my old visitant, irritability, and the Devil told me I should never get it, and so I might as well give it up at once. However, I know him of old as a liar and the father of lies, and pressed on, cast down, yet not destroyed.

'On Friday morning God gave me two precious passages. First, "Come unto Me all ye that labour and are heavy laden, and I will give you rest." Oh, how sweet it sounded to my poor, weary, sin-stricken soul! I almost dared to believe that He did give me rest from inbred sin—the rest of perfect Holiness. But I staggered at the promise through unbelief, and therefore failed to enter in. The second passage consisted of those thrice-blessed words, "Of Him are ye in Christ Jesus, who is made unto us wisdom, righteousness, sanctification, and redemption." But again unbelief hindered me, although I felt as if getting gradually nearer.

'I struggled through the day until a little after six in the evening, when William joined me in prayer. We had a blessed season. While he was saying, "Lord, we open our hearts to receive Thee," that word was spoken to my soul, "Behold, I stand at the door and knock. If any man hear My voice, and open unto Me, I will come in, and sup with him." I felt sure He had long been knocking, and Oh, how I yearned to receive Him as a perfect Saviour! But Oh, the inveterate habit of unbelief! How wonderful that God should have borne so long with me! When we got up from our knees, I lay on the sofa, exhausted with the excitement and effort of the day. William said, " Don't you lay all on the altar?" I replied, " I am sure I do!" Then he said, " And isn't the altar holy?" I replied in the language of the Holy Ghost, " The altar is most holy, and whatsoever toucheth it is holy." Then, said he, " Are you not holy?" I replied with my heart full of emotion and with some faith, " Oh, I think I am!" Immediately the word was given me to confirm my faith. " Now are ye clean through the word which I have spoken unto you." And I took hold—true, with a trembling hand, and not unmolested by the tempter, but I held fast the beginning of my confidence, and it grew stronger, and from that moment I have dared to reckon myself dead indeed unto sin, and alive unto God through Jesus Christ my Lord.

'I did not feel much rapturous joy, but perfect peace, the sweet rest which Jesus promised to the heavy laden. I have understood the Apostle's meaning when he says, " We who believe do enter into rest." This is just descriptive of my state at present. Not that I am not tempted, but I am allowed to know the Devil when he approaches me, and I look to my Deliverer Jesus, and He still gives me rest. Two or three very trying things occurred on Saturday, which at another time would have excited impatience, but I was kept by the power of God through faith unto full Salvation.

'And now what shall I say? "Unto Him who has washed me in His own Blood be glory and dominion for ever and ever," and all within me says "Amen!" Oh! I cannot describe, I have no words to set forth the sense I have of my own utter unworthiness. Satan has met me frequently with my peculiarly aggravated sins, and I have admitted it all. But then I have said, the Lord has not made my sanctification to depend in any measure on my own worthiness or unworthiness, but on the worthiness of my Saviour. He came to seek and to save "that which was lost." "Where sin hath abounded, grace doth much more abound."'

How wonderfully in after years Mrs. Booth explained and led others into this same blessing, we know. Was not, then, the long struggle and agony on her own behalf worth it? Yes, indeed, and it will be so with you when you get this glorious blessing in your soul.

You will have noticed how in struggling for Holiness Mrs. Booth had to fight unbelief. This determination to trust God fully marked her out as strong in faith.

She had this marvellous faith because she obeyed and struggled to throw herself on the Lord; but faith was not *natural* to her any more than it is to you or me.

Often money was short, and she hardly knew how she would be able to feed and clothe her family: this was a sore trial of her faith. On one such occasion she wrote to her mother:—

'We have not at present received as much as our travelling expenses and house rent. I feel a good deal perplexed, and am sometimes tempted to mistrust the Lord. But I will not allow it. Our Father knows!'

Later on we get a sight of her own experience in one of her letters, when she said:—

'I am much tried just now by perplexities of every kind; uncertainty, from a human standpoint, hedges me in on every side. Satan says it is useless trying to steer straight through such a labyrinth; but I am determined to hold on to the promises, come what will. My God is the living God. He sees me, knows me, loves me, cares for me, wants to have me with Him in Glory, as much as He did Abraham, or Paul, or John. If this be true, what have I to fear?'

And again :—

' " Said I not unto thee, that, if thou wouldst believe, thou shouldst see the Salvation of God?" This is a precious word. It has kept my soul alive many a time when Satan has almost overthrown me. " If thou canst believe, all things are possible to thee. Never mind whether anybody else can or cannot. If others are too strong to let Me carry them, if thou art weak enough to throw up all self-effort, and trust Me with thy whole weight, I will carry thee, and thou shalt glorify Me." I know this is the way. Hence the babes go in with the simple and the great sinners, while the reasoners, and the strong, and the proud, and the fearful are shut out.'

Again, to one who was cast down, and tempted to be discouraged because of his failings, she writes :—

' It is well to see them, for how can we take hold of Jesus to mend what we don't see? It is best to know ourselves, but we Salvationists are in danger of erring on the other side. We look too much at ourselves apart from Him who is or would be our righteousness, sanctification, and redemption. Faith in Him as your keeper will do more in five minutes than years of conflict without it.'

Once, in another letter, she gives us a beautiful bit of her own soul's experience on this subject:—

'I had such a view of His love and faithfulness on the journey from Wellingborough, that I thought I would never doubt again about anything. I had the carriage to myself, and such a precious season with the Lord, that the time seemed to fly. As the lightning gleamed around I felt ready to shout, "The chariot of Israel, and the horsemen thereof." Oh, how precious it is when we see as well as believe, but yet more blessed to believe and not see! Lord, work this determined, obstinate, blind, unquestioning, unanswering faith in me and my beloved friend, and let us two dare to trust Thee in the midst of our peculiar trials. As I looked at the waving fields, and grazing sheep, the flashing sky, a Voice said in my soul, "Of what oughtest thou to be afraid? Am I not God? Cannot I supply thy little, tiny needs?" My heart replied, "It is enough, Lord; I will trust Thee, forgive my unbelief."'

IX

LOVE

'The truest love must ever seek the highest good of its object; sometimes even with forgetfulness of important smaller advantages.'—MRS. BOOTH.

THE second great quality in Mrs. Booth's character, as given by the first General, was her love.

'She was *love*,' he says. 'Her whole soul was full of tender, deep compassion. Oh, how she loved, how she pitied the suffering poor! How she longed to put her arms round the sorrowful, and help them!'

'How,' asked Mrs. Booth once, 'are we to put heart into people? Even grace seems to fail to do so in many instances. I think it needs mothers to do this from infancy upwards.'

You will recollect that Mrs. Mumford fostered this 'heart' and love in her little girl; and you will remember how keenly Katie felt, blazing up into wrath at any story of wrong or injury, and ready to sacrifice her life for those she loved. This spirit grew with her. She could not help caring and struggling to help all who needed her. The General often told her in later years that she was killing herself by carrying every one's burdens. Then she would try to leave off for a little, but her heart was too strong, and she could not hold it back.

When but a child, running down the road with her hoop and stick, she saw a drunkard being dragged off to prison by a policeman. All the people were jeering and mocking at the poor friendless wretch. Instantly Katie's pity and love fired up. She dashed across the street, and marched along close by the man's side, so that he might feel that at least one little heart cared for him, and wanted to help him.

To the end of her life she carried this deep, tender pity wherever she went. She loved the poor. 'With all their faults,' she said, 'they have larger hearts than the rich'; and she loved them for it.

Where any one had a warm heart, she could forgive and overlook many mistakes; but with cold, narrow, 'fishy' souls, she had neither sympathy nor patience.

Our Army Mother's help was practical. She did not only give money or pity, but she—so to speak—rolled up her sleeves and helped the suffering herself.

Every sort of suffering and need appealed to her. If an animal was wounded or in pain, she stopped, and herself relieved it as best she could; and to the last, if she saw a horse or any creature being ill-treated, she would not hesitate to rush out and stop the driver, or in some way force him to leave off his cruelty.

She was not only kind and helpful to those she liked, but every living thing that suffered had a claim upon her, and the greater the need the more tender and ready was her help.

Mrs. Booth was a people's woman, and she was never weary of scheming and planning how to help the poor in the most practical way.

'When I see people going wrong,' she said, when but a girl of twelve, 'I must tell the poor things how to manage.'

Dirt and sin, and drink and misery, could not quench this love; it was a part of her very nature. Long, long before Slum Sisters were ever thought of, Mrs. Booth did their work herself, just because she so loved the poor, and longed to help them. You shall read the story in her own words:—

'I remember in one case finding a poor woman lying on a heap of rags. She had just given birth to twins, and there was nobody of any sort to wait upon her. I can never forget the desolation of that room. By her side was a crust of bread and a small lump of lard. "I fancied a bit o' bootter (butter)," the woman remarked apologetically, noticing my eye fall upon the scanty meal, "and my mon, he'd do owt for me he could, bless 'm—he couldna git me iny bootter, so he fitcht me this bit o' lard. Have *you* iver tried lard isted o' bootter? It's *rare good!*" said the poor creature, making me wish I had taken lard for "bootter" all my life, that I might have been the better able to minister to her needs. However, I was soon busy trying to make her a little more comfortable. The babies I washed in a broken pie-dish, the nearest approach to a tub that I could find. And the gratitude of those large eyes, that gazed upon me from out of that wan and shrunken face, can never fade from my memory.'

Before public Meetings took up so much of her time, she delighted in this house-to-house visiting, and went especially for the drunkards, over whom God gave her a wonderful power.

'I used to visit in the evenings,' she says, 'because it was the only part of the day in which I could get away; and, besides, I should not have found the men at home at any other time. I used to ask one drunkard's wife where another lived. They always knew. After getting hold of eight or ten in this way, and getting them to sign the pledge, I used to arrange Cottage Meetings for them, and try to get them saved. They used to let me talk to them in homes where there was not a stick of furniture, and nothing to sit down upon.'

In this way our Army Mother sought and cared for the drunkards long before Drunkards' Brigades were dreamt of.

When, at a later time in her life, she first heard of the wicked and cruel way in which young girls are trapped and drawn into sin, Mrs. Booth's soul was filled with a whirlwind of holy indignation.

'I feel as though I could not rest, but as though I must go and ferret out these monsters myself,' she wrote. 'Almost everybody, notwithstanding the indignation, seems so content with talking. Nobody appears willing to take the responsibility of doing or risking anything. Oh, what a state the world has got into!'

But, deep and practical as was her love in earthly things, her passion for lifting and leading souls into Salvation and Holiness was a thousand times more intense.

'If we only realized, as we ought, the value of souls, we should not live long under it,' she said; and she herself realized it fully enough to make her fight on ceaselessly in spite of intense weakness. 'If it were not for eternity,' she often sighed, 'I should soon give up this life.'

It was love for souls which made her go from town to town, care-worn, weary, often quite unfit to meet the immense congregations which came to hear her.

It was love for souls which kept her sitting for hours at her writing-table, when she should have been resting, trying to help those who turned to her for counsel and direction from every part of the globe.

It was love for souls which gave her many a sleepless night, and chained her to her knees, weeping and pleading, agonizing with God on behalf of the people she was to face the next day.

And this love for souls grew even stronger as death came near. 'Eva,' she exclaimed to one of her daughters, as she lay racked with agonizing pain, 'don't you forget that man with the handcuffs on. Find him. Go to Lancaster Jail; let somebody go with you, and find that man. Tell him that your mother, when she was dying, prayed for him, and that she had a feeling in her heart that God would save him; and tell him, hard as the ten years of imprisonment may be, it will be easier with Christ than it would be without Him.'

She was lying between earth and Heaven, thinking of the joy and peace awaiting her, when it seemed as if she saw the dark face of a heathen woman, and heard the cry, 'Won't you help us?' The old love for perishing souls woke again directly, and she cried, 'Oh, yes, Lord, I will go anywhere to help poor struggling people. I would go on an errand to Hell, if the Lord would promise me that the Devil should not keep me there.'

In one of these last days she sent a dying message to the Officers. 'Tell them,' she said, 'that the only consolation for a Salvationist on his death-bed is to have been a soul-winner. After all my labours I feel I have come far short of the prize of my high calling. Beseech them to redeem their time, for we can do but little at the best.'

A little maid who was a Candidate came into Mrs. Booth's sick-room once as she was speaking, and she called her to her bedside, giving her warning and counsel which every Corps Cadet can take as though spoken to herself:—

'You will be finished with the dishes soon,' she said, 'and you are going to be a Cadet. I have been very pleased with you while you have been here, because you have worked out of sight with a good will, and I think you will make a brave Officer. You will promise me, will you?' she said, as she laid her trembling hand on the girl's head. 'Yes,' was the reply, 'I will,' amid stifled sobs.

'Give me a kiss, then,' said Mrs. Booth. 'Promise me that you will never get spoiled by any unfaithful Officer. If you ever get mixed up with such, do not hide it from Headquarters, but let them know about it, and they will soon move the false away from you. I shan't be here; but, Oh! may God help them to get rid of the wrong. Discernment of spirits! Oh, why should we not have that gift back? It is very necessary.'

Mrs. Booth's whole heart was wrapped up in the spread of The Army, and she was never more of a warrior than when fighting its battles. And The Army needed some one to stand up for it in those days. We who live to-day can hardly fancy the fierce, bitter persecution the early-day Salvationists had to fight through.

Now, even those who dislike and despise us are forced to admit that 'The Army does a great deal of good'; but then it was different, and again and again, both by speech and writing, Mrs. Booth had to defend and stand up for our methods.

'I would not,' she says, after she had spoken too plainly for some rich people who were offended at her words, 'sit down and listen to their abuse of The Salvation Army for all their money. But I did not say a word that I would object to have published upon the housetops. Such, however, is often the spirit of the rich. They think that one must sit and hear whatever they may choose to say, and hold one's breath, because of their money! But, no, I will never be dumb before a golden idol!'

She loved the Uniform: she herself planned that worn by Army women, and always wore her own, rejoicing to be able to give to our people a way of escape from the fashions and extravagances of the world.

She loved the Flag, and was true to its beautiful meaning. She loved to present Colours to the newly-opened Corps, or to parties of Officers going abroad; and when, shortly before she passed away, she changed her room, she begged that the dear Army Flag might be brought in and hung above her bed.

'There,' said The General, 'the Colours are over you now, my darling.'

And she clasped them fondly with her left hand, and traced the motto—'Blood and Fire.'

'Yes,' she said, 'Blood and Fire; that is just what my life has been—a constant and severe fight.'

'It ought to be "Blood and Fire and Victory,"' said The General.

'I'll fight on till I get it,' she answered. 'I won't give in. Next time I see them I shall be above the pain and sorrow for ever.'

But, though at the last she longed to be at rest, it was not easy for her great mother's heart to unloose itself from those she loved, and from the thousands in all lands who looked to her as to a mother.

If you have learnt to love very deeply you will also have to suffer, and her very love made the parting so difficult.

'Oh,' she exclaimed, when speaking of leaving The General and her children, 'mine is such a heart! it seems as if it had got roots all round the world clutching on to one and another, and that it will not let them go! And yet You can take care of them, Lord, better than I could. I do, I do believe! O Eternal Father, Shepherd of the sheep, do Thou look after my little flock!'

'Amen,' we who read these lines may say; adding to her prayer, 'And give us that same heart and love which made her life of such mighty power.'

X

THE WARRIOR

'Fighting is hard work, whatever sort of fighting it is. You cannot fight without wounds of body, heart, or soul.'—MRS. BOOTH.

'LASTLY,' said The General in that same beautiful tribute to our Army Mother that I have already quoted from, 'she was a *warrior.* She liked the fight. She was not one who said to others, "Go," but "Here, let *me* go"; and when there was the necessity she said, "I *will* go!" I never knew her flinch until her poor body compelled her to lie on one side.'

Our Army Mother was, indeed, before all things a warrior; she fought bravely and unceasingly her whole life through.

In thought and purpose she was independent, and dared to stand out for what she felt right. Cowardice, in her opinion, was one of the commonest and most subtle sins of the day, and she had no patience with those who dared not say 'No,' and feared to stand alone.

She thought for herself, and though always eager to hear and learn as much as possible from others, yet she was not carried away by their opinions, but carefully weighed and considered their arguments, and then formed her own judgments.

Mrs. Booth strove earnestly for doctrine.

'Let us take care,' she said, in The Army's early days, 'what Gospel we preach. Let us mind our doctrine.'

And again :—

'We must stick to the form of sound words, for there is more in it than appears on the surface. "Glory be to the Father, to the Son, and the Holy Ghost," was the theology of our forefathers, and I am suspicious of all attempts to mend it.'

And once more :—

'Let us beware of wrong doctrine, come through whomsoever it may. Holy men make sad mistakes. "Well, but," say some, "is not a person who holds wrong views with a right heart better than a person with right views and a wrong heart?" Yes, so far as his personal state before God is concerned, but not in his influence on man. My charity must extend to those likely to be deceived or ruined by his doctrines as well as to him.'

Mrs. Booth's whole life was a continual fight against sin—sin of all kinds. Whether her Meeting was held for the very lowest and roughest, or whether rows of clergy and lawyers, and lords and ladies sat to listen, it made no difference to her. She attacked sin, and went straight at the very heart-sins of the people in front of her.

'We need great grace,' she says in the midst of her wonderful West-End campaign, where even princes and princesses came to hear her. 'I think the Lord never enabled me to be more plain and faithful. As a lady in high circles said to me, "We never heard this sort of Gospel before." No, poor things, they are sadly deceived.'

Drink, too, was another evil which Mrs. Booth fought against during the whole of her life. She began, as you remember, when a girl by being secretary of the 'Band of Love' of those days.

In the early days of their engagement The General was strongly advised to take a little wine for the sake of his health. Our Army Mother wrote him a long letter, showing him how false and foolish such advice was, and ending with :—

'I have had it recommended to me scores of times, but I am fully and for ever settled on the physical side of the question.*

'It is a subject on which I am most anxious you should be thorough. I have far more hope for your health *because* you abstain, than I should if you took wine. Flee the detestable thing as you would a serpent; be a teetotaller in principle and practice.'

Though, as we have seen, full of boundless faith and pity for the drunkard, Mrs. Booth attacked the makers and sellers of drink unmercifully. She says, on one occasion :—

'By your peace of conscience on a dying bed; by the eternal destinies of your children, by your care for never-dying souls; by the love you owe your Saviour, I beseech you *banish the drink*.

'Tell me no more of charity towards brewers, distillers, and publicans. Your false charity to these has already consigned millions to an untimely Hell! . . . Arise,

* That means taking it for the sake of health.—Ed.

Christians, arise, and fight this foe! You and you alone are able, for your God will fight for you!'

Another thing for which our Army Mother fought, and which to-day we owe in great measure to her efforts, is the position to which women have been lifted as speakers and teachers in God's work. She first, as we have seen, opened the way herself; and then she left it open, encouraging and helping tens of thousands of simple, holy women all round the world to follow in her steps.

She had a tough battle to wage. All classes wrote and spoke against women being allowed to stand and speak for God in the open air or in public halls; but, strong in faith and courage, convinced that she had Divine authority for what she did, our Army Mother fought on, arguing, writing, preaching on the matter. Now to-day there is scarcely a land where The Army bonnet is not known and loved, nor where Army women cannot gain a crowd of respectful listeners.

Now I am going to show you some of the hindrances in spite of which our Army Mother fought on.

The first of these hindrances was the burden which God allowed Mrs. Booth to carry all through her life—a weak and suffering body. She said, when her life was drawing to its close, that suffering seemed to have been her special lot, and that she could scarcely remember a day in her life when she had been wholly free from pain.

'I don't care about my body,' she exclaimed when lying in her last illness. 'It has been a poor old troublesome affair. I shall be glad for it to be sealed up. It is time it was. Oh, I have dragged it wearily about.'

Most women suffering as she did, with a weak spine, heart disease, and over-strained nerves, would have lived the life of an invalid. But the warrior spirit within forced her body along. Scores of times she has gone from her bed to the Meeting, and then, exhausted and fainting with the effort, has had to be almost carried home. But she had done her work, and sent the arrow of conviction into hundreds of hearts.

Writing after one special strain of work and anxiety, she says:—

'The excitement made me worse than I have been for two years. My heart was really alarming, and for two days I could hardly bear any clothes to touch me. This has disheartened me again as to my condition. But God reigns, and He will keep me alive as long as He needs me.'

Another of her hindrances, and one which was almost more difficult to overcome than weakness of body, was depression.

I wonder if you know what that is? If so, it will help you to realize that Mrs. Booth had to fight it also.

The Devil seemed allowed to try and test her faith to the uttermost, and at times to blot out all peace and glory from her soul. During one such time of darkness she writes:—

'I know I ought not, of all saints, or sinners either, to be depressed. I know it dishonours my Lord, grieves His Spirit, and injures me greatly; and I would fain hide from everybody to prevent their seeing it. But I cannot help it. I have struggled hard, more than any one knows, for a long time against it. Sometimes I have literally held myself, head and heart and hands, and waited for the floods to pass over me.'

But our Army Mother did not give up working for God, and sit down in despair, because she was thus tried. One day, just before leaving for a great West-End Meeting, in which God made her words as a sharp two-edged sword, she wrote this to one of her children :—

'I have been very much depressed since you left—more so than usual. It is of no use reasoning with myself when these fits of despondency are on me. I must hold on and fight my passage through; and when I get to Heaven the light and joy will be all the greater. If I dared give up working I should do so a hundred times over; but I *dare* not.'

Another and constant hindrance which our Army Mother had to fight for the greater part of her life was poverty. It was so difficult, many times, to make two ends meet. She had, during many years of her life, no regular money coming in on which to depend, and during that time it was a constant struggle to have her children properly cared for and give them the needed education.

But most of all did our Army Mother show herself a warrior in her own Salvation campaigns. In those early days there were no praying Soldiers and Sergeants to be had to deal with the penitents—no one, either, to lead her singing, scarcely even to keep the doors or take up the collection. She would arrive in a town absolutely alone. A hall had been taken in which she was to speak, and she would hire a tiny lodging, or stay in whatever home would receive her, and set to work. We can scarcely understand the loneliness of her position. Here was a proof of her mighty faith in God.

She began these solitary campaigns when her sixth child was but a few weeks old, and God most wonderfully owned her labours. At one place she saw one hundred grown-up people and two hundred children come to her penitent-form in six days. But it was a fearful battle.

'I have a comfortable little cot to stay in,' she writes to her mother from one such battle-field, 'very small and humble; but it is clean and quiet; and when I feel nervous no one knows the value of quietness. I have felt it hard work lately. Many a time have I longed to be where the weary are at rest.'

At Margate, some years later, she commenced her Meetings without knowing a single person in the place. For some weeks she had not even a helper in the Prayer Meetings, nor one who would give out a song for her. Mrs. Booth could not sing herself, and there was often an awkward pause before any one would be willing to pitch her tune. 'If only,' she said when The Army was fairly on its feet, 'I had been able to command a dozen reliable people such as I could have anywhere now, I think I could have done almost anything.'

Even more wonderful was her experience at Brighton.

The Dome, a great building holding three thousand people, had been taken for her Meetings.

'I can never forget my feelings,' says this Soldier-saint, 'as I stood upon the platform and looked upon the people, realizing that among them all there was no one to help me. When I commenced the Prayer Meeting, for which I should think quite nine hundred remained, Satan said to me, as I came down from the platform according to my custom, "You will never ask such people as these to come and kneel down here? You will only make a fool of yourself if you do." I felt stunned for a moment; but I answered, "Yes, I shall. I shall not make it any easier for them than for the others. If they do not realize their sins enough to be willing to come and kneel here, they will not be of much use to the kingdom."'

The Lord set His seal upon Mrs. Booth's faith and courage, for the first to volunteer were two old gentlemen, both over seventy years of age; and she had ten or twelve at the mercy-seat before the Meeting ended.

Writing from Portsmouth, she tells the same story of loneliness and victory:—

'You say, "How do you get on personally?" Oh, I never was so hampered for help in every way in all my life! The most able man I have keeps a milliner's shop, and the one that opens for me generally is an overseer; so their attention is divided and the time limited. Pray for me. I never needed your prayers so much. This is a dreadfully wicked place.'

Yet during the seventeen weeks of her stay some six hundred names were taken, many of them wonderful trophies of God's mercy.

Having lived such a warrior's life, you think, very likely, that the death-bed experience of our Army Mother would be all peace and glory. But no. Right down into the Valley she needed to use the Sword of the Spirit and the Shield of Faith, for to the last Satan was allowed to test and try her.

But she fought on!

'One of my hardest lessons,' she said in her last hours, 'has been the difference between faith and realization; and if I have had to conquer all through life by naked faith, I can only expect it to be the same now. All our enemies have to be conquered by *faith*, not realization; and is it not so with the last enemy, death? Yes, if it please the Lord that I should go down into the dark valley without any realization, simply knowing that I am His, and He is mine, I am quite willing—I accept it.'

This is the faith that made our Army Mother and all the Bible saints such conquerors. It is the secret of their victory—the faith without which it is impossible to please God, and for which we all need to pray, 'Lord, increase our faith.'

XI

LAST DAYS

'As I look back on life I do not remember the houses I have lived in, the people that I have known, the things of passing interest at the moment. They are all gone. There is nothing stands out before my mind as of any consequence, but the work I have done for God and Eternity.' —Mrs. Booth.

If The General and those who loved our Army Mother best had been able to choose for her, they would most likely have said: 'Let her live and fight and work on, up to within a few days of her promotion to Glory. Let the call come quickly and painlessly, as it has come to others in our ranks.'

But the Lord, who loved her more than we did, saw fit to send to her two and a half years of ever-increasing weariness and suffering. For long months she lay on the very bank of the River, longing for the messenger of Death to carry her across. Those who loved her could not tell why the

Lord sent her this last fiery trial; they could only bow with her, and say, 'Thy will be done.'

It was in February, 1888, that Mrs. Booth, who was anxious about her health, went to consult a great doctor and get his opinion. She was alone, for no one had thought her illness was so serious. She asked him to tell her the truth—all through her life, as you know, she wanted the truth; and after a little hesitation he told her.

The truth was the saddest that she could hear. That dreadful illness—cancer—through which she had so tenderly nursed her own dear mother, had come to her, and in the doctor's opinion she had much suffering to pass through, and only two or, at the most, three years longer to live. Mrs. Booth listened calmly, thanked the doctor, and then, getting once more into the cab, drove home all alone.

It was a dark journey. The War needed her. The General needed her. Her children needed her. And yet the sentence of Death had been passed upon her, and she must soon leave them all. What did she do? I think you can guess.

She knelt down in the cab, and in prayer

committed to God, in a new and deeper way than ever before, her own body, and her dear ones and the work He had given her to do.

At last the cab stopped before her own door, and The General came out to meet her.

'I shall never forget that meeting in this world, or the next,' he says. 'I had been watching for the cab, and had run out to meet her and help her up the steps. She tried to smile on me through her tears; but, drawing me into the room, soon told me, bit by bit, what the doctor had said. I sat down speechless. She rose from her seat, and came and knelt beside me, saying: "Do you know what was my first thought? That I should not be there to nurse you in your last hour."

'I was stunned. I felt as if the whole world were coming to a standstill. Opposite me, on the wall, was a picture of Christ on the cross. I thought I could understand it then, as never before. She talked to me like an angel; she talked as she had never talked before. I could say little or nothing. I could only kneel with her and try to pray.

That very same night The General was

to leave London for some great Meetings in Holland, and Mrs. Booth would not hear of his changing his plans and remaining with her.

'The War must go on' was her thought, even when all her family stood stunned and heart-broken around her, unwilling to leave her even for a moment.

Two years later, when but a few more days of suffering remained to her, a last message from her lips reached us as Self-Denial Week began. 'The War must go on' was one of its sentences.

'The War must go on' had been as her motto, lived out in all the long, long months that lay between. Instead of immediately laying aside her work, when the doctors gave their dreadful judgment, and beginning to think only of herself, she went on with it as long as her increasing weakness allowed.

But step by step the disease grew worse. First she was forced to give up Meetings and public work. Then it became impossible for her to use her right hand, and she was therefore obliged to give up her correspondence, though she still continued to dictate her letters, and learnt also to write with her left hand.

Soon her daily drives became too tiring, and by and by she went out of the house into the little garden for the last time; and then for the concluding twelve months of her life she was a prisoner in her room, lying in constant suffering.

But during these long months the greatest joy and relief that could come to her was to hear of some fresh victory or triumph for the Kingdom of Jesus. Her interest in The Army and her love for the people were as keen as ever, and War Councils were held and new developments planned in her chamber, and much of The General's Darkest England Scheme for the poor and outcast was thought out and decided upon beside her sick bed.

Again and again, too, Mrs. Booth would receive deputations of Officers of different classes and from various countries in which The Army was at work, who came to Clacton-on-Sea, where the last fifteen months of her life were spent, to listen to her words of advice and inspiration.

There were no Corps Cadets in those days; but our Army Mother left some specially beautiful words about the Juniors, to which I must refer.

When she was told by the Officer then in charge of our Junior Work in England that the children loved and prayed continually for her, she smiled.

'The thought of the little ones,' says some one who was there, 'brought our beloved Army Mother wholly out of herself and her pain and weariness.'

'A very choice branch of the work,' she said. 'I have often told Emma that I hoped when I was too old for public work God would let me end where I began—with the children. But it seems that it is not to be so.'

'Give the children,' she went on, in reply to the messages they had sent, 'my dear love, and tell them that if there had been a Salvation Army when I was ten I should have been a Soldier then, as I am to-day.

'Never allow yourself to be discouraged in your work. I know you must meet with many discouragements; but I am sure the Spirit of God works mightily on little children long before grown people think they are able to understand.'

Again and again during that last year of awful suffering it seemed as if Mrs. Booth were about to leave us; but then she would revive, and come back to endure more weeks and months of agony.

But at last, on October 4, 1890, all could see that she was on the brink of the River, and even those who loved her the most tenderly could not wish to hold her back.

'O Emma, let me go, darling,' she whispered; and hearing the reply, 'Yes, we will, we will,' she said, 'Now! Yes, Lord, come, Oh, come!'

The singing of The Army songs seemed to comfort her; and once she raised her suffering arm, and pointed to the text, '*My grace is sufficient for thee*,' which hung on the wall. It was lifted down and placed at the foot of her bed, so that her eyes could often rest on it during those last hours.

'Soon after noon,' says the present General, 'I felt that the deepening darkness of the Valley was closing around my dear mother, and a little later I took my last farewell. Her lips moved, and she gave me one look of unspeakable tenderness and trust which will live with me for ever. Again we sang:—

My mistakes His free grace doth cover,
My sins He doth wash away;
These feet which shrink and falter
Shall enter the Gates of Day.

And, holding her hand, The General gave her up to God. It was a solemn and wonderful scene.'

The Chief of the Staff and Mrs. Bramwell Booth, Mrs. Booth-Tucker, and the Commander, and her three daughters, Marian, Eva, and Lucy, knelt round the bed, upon which were placed photographs of the other members of her family who were unavoidably absent. Near to her stood her faithful nurse, Captain Carr, and others of the household, the dear General bowing over his beloved wife and companion in life's long strife, and giving her up to the keeping of the Father.

One by one the members of the family tenderly embraced her; then a gleam of recognition passed over the brightening countenance as The General bent over her. Their eyes met—the last kiss of love on earth, the last word till the Morning, and without a movement the breathing gently ceased, and a warrior laid down her sword to receive her crown.

. . . .

You may have heard of those wonderful days from Tuesday morning till Sunday night, when the coffin containing the precious remains of our Army Mother lay at the Congress Hall, Clapton, and when more than fifty thousand people came to have a last look at her dear face.

A piece of glass had been let into the plain oak coffin. It was just large enough to show the head and shoulders, and she lay as if in a sweet sleep.

You wonder if many came merely from curiosity. Some did, of course, but most of the people came because her life and example and words had been so blessed to their souls; and they came as they would come to look at the dead face of their own mother. It was the most wonderful tribute to a woman's life and words that London had ever seen.

For all kinds of people came—rich and poor, good and bad, people of many different religions, and many with no religion at all. Working-men came in their dinner-hour, with their tools on their backs and tears in their eyes; mothers lifted up their little children to look at the one who had taught them the way of life; and, best of all, by the side of her coffin knelt many a wanderer and backslider to give themselves afresh to God.

More than one poor girl went direct from

the Congress Hall to the Rescue Homes, to begin to live 'as she would have wished'; and the Cadets on guard were all the time dealing with drunkards and helping those who desired to begin from thenceforth to live a new and different life.

Even to-day, twenty-four years later, we often meet those who date their conversion, or their first step in the Narrow Way, from their look at that face lying in its simple coffin.

One of Mrs. Booth's own grandchildren, Mary, the present General's second daughter, looks back to that scene as the time when God in an unmistakable manner sealed her as His. She was only five years old as she knelt by the coffin, but nevertheless she decided there, in her childish consecration, like Ruth of old, that 'Thy people shall be my people, and thy God my God'; and in the spirit of this consecration she lives to-day.

. . . .

In order that some of the crowds who wished to share in the funeral service might be present, the largest hall in London, the Olympia, was taken. Twenty-six thousand people filled it; and though it was, of course, impossible for them all to hear, they followed the service given on printed papers with reverent sympathy.

The coffin was carried down the immense hall by Officers; The General and his family followed.

Those who arranged for this last mighty gathering remembered that Mrs. Booth, when with us, was never happy to leave a Meeting unless it had been brought to a point, and something definite had been done; and therefore, when the songs and prayers and readings were over, the huge crowd was asked to kneel and make a solemn covenant with God.

It was a beautiful covenant, and ended with these words:—

'And now, in this solemn hour, and in the presence of death, I come again to Thy footstool, and make this covenant with Thee.'

Then all who had made the covenant from their hearts rose and sang together:—

Just as I am Thou dost receive,
Dost welcome, pardon, cleanse, relieve,
Because Thy promise I believe,
O Lamb of God, I come!

It was just such an ending to the wonderful service as our Army Mother would have chosen had she been still on earth with us.

. . . .

The next morning was dry and bright. 'I shall ask God to give you a fine day for my funeral, Emma, so that you mayn't take cold,' our Army Mother had said, for she was ever thoughtful for others; and her prayer was answered, for though the white mist crept up from the river to the Embankment, where the procession was forming up, there was no rain nor wind.

Tens of thousands of our dear Soldiers would gladly have sacrificed a day's work in order to follow in the funeral procession of one they so dearly loved; but, so as not to gather too large a crowd, only Officers were allowed in the march, which passed through countless throngs of people from International Headquarters to Abney Park Cemetery, a distance of about five miles.

All along the route the crowds stood in dense masses, and roofs, windows, and every nook and corner were packed with human beings. Nothing had been seen like it, said the police, since the Duke of Wellington's funeral, forty years before.

It was a wonderful march. I wish you

could have seen it! Sometimes it seemed as if every one was weeping; and when the open hearse, with its plain oak coffin, crowned by The Army bonnet and well-worn Bible, passed, all heads were bared, all voices hushed, and tears filled all eyes.

The General, standing alone in his open carriage all along the long, sad way, must have felt that he had the people's sympathy and love with him in his grief, for scores of heartfelt 'God bless you's!' came from lips that are unused to such words.

And at last the yellow evening sun shone out as the great procession reached the gates of Abney Park Cemetery and wound towards the open grave.

Only a part of the mighty throng could hear The General's beautiful words, so strong and yet so tender, from which I have already quoted, but all joined in the song, 'Rock of Ages,' which seemed to roll up to the heavens themselves.

Several leading Officers and members of The General's own family prayed and spoke, wonderfully upheld in spite of their deep grief and the strain of the last days. And then by the open grave the present General led all hearts to make a fresh consecration, the whole assembly promising, with God's help, that they would be

'Faithful to Thee, faithful to one another, and faithful to a dying world, till we meet our beloved Mother in the Morning. Amen.'

. . . .

If ever you are in Abney Park Cemetery you should visit her grave. It is very simple. Around the little piece of earth runs a grey stone, with these words carved on it:—

CATHERINE BOOTH,

MOTHER OF THE SALVATION ARMY

More than Conqueror, through Him that loved us, and gave Himself for all the world and for you.

Do you also follow Christ?

and above are two small beds of flowers.

Do many people go to see it? you wonder.

Oh, yes. All round it a path is worn in the grass, made by the tread of many feet; for mothers bring their boys and girls to see it, and tell them what a mother she was, and men and women of all creeds and races pause beside it, and remember.

Many Officers, too—from distant lands, and speaking strange tongues you could not understand — come to The Army Mother's grave when they visit our shores. For she was their Mother as well as ours, they say.

They kneel beside the stone, and spell out the name, and then they consecrate themselves afresh to God and the needs of the heathen lands, and they claim His grace to follow in her steps.

For our Army Mother is not dead. True, her body lies in the quiet grave at Abney Park, and her spirit is in Heaven; but her life and influence still live among us, her words are treasured, and our greatest prayer and desire for the girls and wives and mothers in our ranks is that they may live to be worthy daughters of Catherine Booth.

DATES IN MRS. BOOTH'S LIFE

1829. January 17th. Catherine Mumford born at Ashbourne, Derby.
1829. April 10th. William Booth born at Nottingham.
1843. Catherine has to leave school owing to severe illness.
1844. Refuses to be engaged to her cousin.
1845. Is converted.
1846 Seems likely to go into consumption.
1850. Takes Sunday class of elder girls.
1851. June. Miss Mumford hears Mr. Booth preach; later meets him at a friend's house.
1852. May 15th. They are engaged to be married.
1855. June 16th. The wedding.
1857. Mrs. Booth speaks to a children's meeting on Temperance.
1859. She starts work among drunkards. She writes her first pamphlet on woman's right to preach.
1860. Mrs. Booth speaks for the first time in public.
1861. Mr. and Mrs. Booth break up their home in the north, and come to London, choosing an evangelistic life.
1864. Mrs. Booth begins to hold Evangelistic campaigns apart from her husband.
1864. July. East End Mission begun.
1868. First Headquarters established.
1869. Mrs. Booth's wonderful Brighton campaign.
1870. East London Mission becomes the 'Christian Mission.'
1871. Mrs. Booth publishes her first book.
1877. Christian Mission becomes 'The Salvation Army.'
1878. The uniform is chosen.
1886. First Self-Denial Week.
1888. February. Mrs. Booth learns that she is suffering from cancer.
1888. June 21st. Mrs. Booth speaks in public for the last time (at the City Temple).
1889. August. She goes to Clacton-on-Sea.
1890. October 4th. Mrs. Booth is promoted to Glory.
1890. October 6th. Her body brought to Congress Hall, Clapton.
1890. October 11th. Funeral at Abney Park.

CPSIA information can be obtained at www.ICGtesting.com
Printed in the USA
LVOW101844230912

299898LV00001B/46/P

9 780880 191128